Communication
Criticism

RHETORIC AND SOCIETY

edited by Herbert W. Simons
Temple University

EDITORIAL BOARD

This series will publish a broad-based collection of advanced texts and innovative works encompassing rhetoric in the civic arena, in the arts and media, in the academic disciplines, and in everyday cultural practices.

Books in this series:

Control and Consolation in American Culture and Politics: Rhetorics of Therapy
Dana L. Cloud

Communication Criticism: Developing Your Critical Powers
Jodi R. Cohen

Analyzing Everyday Texts: Discourse, Rhetoric, and Social Perspectives
Glenn F. Stillar

JODI R. COHEN

Communication Criticism

Developing Your Critical Powers

Rhetoric & Society

SAGE Publications
International Educational and Professional Publisher
Thousand Oaks London New Delhi

For information:

SAGE Publications, Inc.
2455 Teller Road
Thousand Oaks, California 91320
E-mail: order@sagepub.com

SAGE Publications Ltd.
6 Bonhill Street
London EC2A 4PU
United Kingdom

SAGE Publications India Pvt. Ltd.
M-32 Market
Greater Kailash I
New Delhi 110 048 India

Printed in the United States of America

Library of Congress Cataloging-in-Publication Data

Main entry under title:

Cohen, Jodi R.
  Communication criticism: Developing your critical
powers / by Jodi R. Cohen.
    p. cm. — (Rhetoric and society ; vol. 2.)
  Includes bibliographical references (p.) and index.
  ISBN 0-7619-0629-0 (acid-free paper). — ISBN 0-7619-0630-4 (pbk.:
  acid-free paper)
    1. Communication criticism. I. Title. II. Series: Rhetoric and
society (Thousand Oaks, Calif.) ; v. 2.
  P96.C76C64 1998
  302.2—dc21   97-45334

98 99 00 01 02 03 10 9 8 7 6 5 4 3 2 1

Acquiring Editor:	Margaret Seawell
Editorial Assistant:	Renée Piernot
Production Editor:	Michele Lingre
Production Assistant:	Lynn Miyata
Typesetter/Designer:	Danielle Dillahunt
Indexer:	Wiil Ragsdale
Cover Designer:	Candice Harman
Print Buyer:	Anna Chin

This book is for my family:
I love you.

This book was written with considerable and
considerate conceptual advice from
Herb Simons and Mark Pollock, and editorial
help from June Hannah and Dorothy Owens.
I thank you.

Contents

Series Editor's Introduction

Many years ago I had a colleague at Temple University whose elective course in General Semantics closed each semester on the first day of registration with well over a hundred students enrolled. Harry Weinberg used no multimedia in his course (in fact, I believe the term hadn't yet been invented). He had a weak speaking voice, so that students in the back of the room had to strain to hear him. And he had a rather severe speech impediment. But Harry Weinberg was, by virtually all accounts, a master teacher.

Harry Weinberg excelled as a teacher for many of the usual reasons, including great personal warmth, caring for his subject matter, and commitment to his students. Professor Weinberg also took extraordinary steps to communicate complex ideas clearly. On any given lecture period, he made sure to limit himself to a very few concepts and principles. Then he would illustrate these concepts and principles at great length, often building on examples that he'd introduced in previous periods. And he would also try to anticipate the questions and concerns of his students.

On reading Jodi Cohen's *Communication Criticism: Developing Your Critical Powers*, I was reminded of Harry Weinberg's General Semantics class. Cohen has one overriding goal for you, her students: to empower you as listeners, readers and viewers of communicated messages. Toward that end she introduces a rather limited set of ideas per chapter, but the ideas build on one another so that by the middle of the book, Professor Cohen will be able to say, in ways that you will be able to understand "Once comfortable with the pentad you should gain a more practical understanding of the idea that people construct reality with communication. People interpellate themselves into ideologies through dramatic transactions."

This a mouthful, isn't it? In fact, many advanced graduate students in communication studies might find the concepts which I have italized extremely difficult. But because Jodi Cohen is a master teacher—because, for example, she has taken pains to anticipate your difficulties with Kenneth Burke's concept of the pentad and responded to them with clear explanations and detailed examples, you should find the concepts eminently digestible by the time you've chewed your way through them.

For any communicative act or artifact, *Communication Criticism: Developing Your Critical Powers* invites its readers to consider three basic questions: (1) How does the "message" (i.e., the act or artifact) fulfill the creator's purpose? (2) Does the "message" present the world, and/or ideas about the world, truthfully and ethically? (3) How does the message shape identities, ideas, and actions? Variants of these same three questions are found at the end of nearly all chapters, so that whether you are thinking about verbal style or film and video editing, you'll have these questions to guide you. And Professor Cohen will illustrate how these questions may be answered, oftentimes with references to examples or studies of popular culture.

The most distinctive feature of this book is its blending of classical rhetoric with postmodernism. This is controversial, and your instructor may wish to challenge Professor Cohen when she says in the Preface that "The goals of much postmodern scholarship, often considered 'radical' are for the most part consistent with the goals of traditional rhetoric: to gain power over our lives by thinking critically about communication."

This is a provocative statement and, I think, a profound one. It's provocative because we academics are often prone either to cling to tradition in the face of all newcomers, or to disparage the old in the name of progress, Wasn't it John Lennon who told us that "what's old is what's new"?

That's profound.

Herbert W. Simons
Series Editor

Preface

■ *Author's Notes on the Philosophy and Design of the Book*

Most books on critical thinking focus on research methodology or how to write formal, critical essays. My objective in writing this book is to help the reader, who may take only one communication course or read only one book about communication in their lifetime, to think critically about everyday communication.

The book draws on a wide range of communication forms, including novels, theatre, political speeches, films, and everyday conversations. It is, therefore, an appropriate guide to thinking critically about all communication. In an effort to encompass a full range of communication, the book presents concepts for critical thinking that have been developed in a variety of fields and perspectives. A teacher's manual, available from Sage, addresses the ways *Communication Criticism: Developing Your Critical Powers* may be adapted to a range of courses and students.

Although the book is broad in its presentation of communication forms and theories and intended for readers who adhere to a range of philosophies, it gains coherence from the traditional principles of "rhetoric." Rhetoric was once a branch of philosophy dedicated to the study of oral, public communication. The field of rhetoric has changed, incorporating ideas from fields as diverse as critical social studies and social psychology. It has also broadened its subjects to include all forms of communication. The classical study of rhetoric provides the book with its goals and structure, which are herein synthesized with contemporary-critical approaches to popular culture.

The classical goals of rhetoric are attached to the role of persuasive speaking in the development of Greek democracy. Twenty-five hundred years ago public speaking was the primary means of shaping public opinion and therefore essential to the entire democratic decision-making process. The formal study of rhetoric was important to educating the citizens of ancient Greece in how to influence others through persuasive speaking skills. Primarily developed as a practical study, the knowledge of rhetoric also protected citizens from the undue influence of others.

Today, or 2,500 years ago, the rhetorical view of communication attempts to give people the power to affect their own lives. In contemporary American education, vestiges of the practical art of rhetoric are found in public speaking and composition courses. Some academic programs—most notably Speech Communication, Writing, English Literature, Film and Media Studies—offer courses in critical communication skills that attend to the effects communication may have on particular audiences. Many of these programs are grounded in the traditional, practical art of rhetoric.

The classical goals of rhetoric are consistent with the perspectives and pedagogical needs of the 21st century. In the 1990s, most academic disciplines include at least a handful of scholars who believe communication has a significant, if not defining, role in creating reality. Rather than assume the world is endowed with meaning and truth that is mediated through communication, contemporary philosophies tend to blur the borders between reality, language, thought, action, and identity. Postmodern thinking, a philosophical movement evident in the arts, sciences, and humanities, considers communication to be the source, if not the essence, of who we are, what we know, and what we do. The goals of much postmodern scholarship, often considered "radical," are for the most part consistent with the goals of traditional rhetoric: to gain power over our lives by thinking critically about communication.

The structure of this book, influenced by the structure of traditional rhetorical studies, integrates concepts from a variety of critical fields. Unit One introduces the reader to the central role of communication in all that we do, and to a process for thinking critically about communication. The critical process is based on the neo-Aristotelian model of rhetorical criticism that emerged from Cornell University in the 1920s and was at that time central to distinguishing the study of oral from written communication. The critical method takes the critical thinker through three steps: an analysis of the communication context, an interpretation of the audience making meaning, and a judgment about that meaning. Critical thinking is described as linear and systematic but in actuality it is a simultaneous and creative process.

Units Two through Six organize concepts for critical thinking according to whether they focus on language, structure, reasoning, character, or emotion. Each unit opens with a chapter on the neo-Aristotelian approach to the topic, followed by chapters that address contemporary-postmodern concepts and broaden critical powers from "public speech" to "popular communication."

Unit Two presents concepts for unraveling the role of language in meaning, beginning with the classical concept of "style" in Chapter 3, followed by "semiology" and "metaphors."

Unit Three presents a variety of concepts best adapted to studying the structure of communication, beginning with a chapter on the neo-Aristotelian theory of "organization." The chapters in this unit also address the principles of visual "editing," "narrative," and "dramatism."

Units Four, Five, and Six address what was traditionally studied under the heading of "invention," that is, reasoning, character, and emotion. The book offers three ways to think critically about reasoning in communication: "rhetorical argument," "field-dependent argument," and "narrative rationality." The chapters on character and emotion cover the traditional concepts of "ethos" and "pathos," as well as more contemporary explanations of "identification," "second persona," and the psychoanalytic notion of "desire."

These units present a vocabulary for critical thinking in parallel format. Each unit introduces the topic and briefly considers the relationship of the topic under consideration to who we are, what we know, and what we do. A variety of positions is presented, but none is argued. Each chapter presents, explains, applies, and discusses the strengths and weaknesses of a critical concept. The text is not advocating the use of some concepts over others but suggests that their usefulness depends upon the critic's assumptions and questions.

The critic's assumptions and questions are the focus of the final unit, which summarizes the book by moving critical thinking into reflection.

This unit suggests the critical process may begin in a variety of ways, but ultimately critics should use the critical vocabulary in ways that are best suited to their questions and assumptions. The critical questions and concepts presented throughout the book are reviewed within different theoretical perspectives, and their implications to critical powers are addressed.

The content of this book broadens, sometimes stretches, the traditional study of rhetoric. Public communication is no longer limited to public speaking. The introduction and Chapter 1 make it very clear that, however influenced by traditional rhetorical approaches to criticism, this text is concerned with all communication. The book makes room for critical concepts associated with Michel Foucault and Karl Marx, within the classical method of critical reflection. For instance, the epistemological and institutional-economic contexts of communication are considered, along with the traditional analysis of the "rhetorical situation." During the interpretive phase of criticism, the reader is encouraged to apply a variety of theoretical concepts. Similarly, the evaluative phase, as herein presented, invites critical questions about whether the communication is effective, truthful, and ethical, as it also probes the ideological implications of communication to social power and cultural identities.

In review, the lay critic needs to know two important bodies of information that are rarely found in one source: the fundamental principles of communication, and how these principles have been, and can be, adapted to thinking critically about how people make meaning. The traditional study of rhetoric remains relevant to the task because its goals are consistent with contemporary concerns and it provides the most thorough, systematic, and accessible framework for the beginning student. In addition, the classical approach is flexible enough to integrate different communication philosophies and theoretical concepts into its framework.

Jodi R. Cohen
Ithaca College, Ithaca, NY

UNIT 1

AN INTRODUCTION TO
COMMUNICATION AND CRITICISM

We never escape communication or its effects. Typically we use the radio alarm to ease us into another day. If we remain in bed, struggling to awaken, the sounds of the radio may mingle with the images of our dreams. The flash of symbols that move through us during our waking moments shape our thoughts and actions: television, newspapers, food packages, magazine articles, advertisements, billboards, bumper stickers, road signs, cartoons, a book, a set of instructions, phone calls, mail, electronic mail and discussions, spontaneous conversations, and movies, to mention only some of the more obvious. The influx and influence of symbols is compounded throughout the days, the weeks, and the years of our lives. My purpose in writing this book is to help readers realize the power of such everyday communication and develop the power to shape meaning through communication criticism.

The hero of Robert James Waller's novel, *The Bridges of Madison County* (1995), is a photographer who does not like his photographs to be analyzed because "analysis destroys wholes. Some things, magic

1

things, are meant to stay whole. If you look at the pieces they go away" (p. 39). Most communication is similarly magical in that it can shape values, feelings, and actions while concealing the symbolic, and often arbitrary, processes of construction. Unlike the photographic artist, who creates meaning through the mystery of art, the critical artist recreates meaning by unraveling the mysteries of art. The person who thinks critically about communication can expose meaning in the same way that Dorothy's little dog, Toto, exposes the Wizard of Oz. Recall that Toto pulls away the curtain and reveals the tricks that make the wizard seem powerful to his believers. Communication can lose some of its mystery and power under the scrutiny of critical thinking. The critical thinker is free to choose among meanings and thereby gain some power over them.

Most of the chapters in this book are dedicated to a vocabulary that can guide us through the critical process. This unit lays the foundation by explaining the claims stated in the preceding paragraphs. The first chapter explains the power of communication in shaping who we are, what we know, and what we do. The second chapter outlines a systematic process for thinking critically about communication: description, interpretation, and evaluation. While the explication of critical thinking may seem too cumbersome for everyday thinking, it does offer a vocabulary for developing and justifying the kinds of judgments we make about communication every day. I recommend the process be used as an ideal guide and as a reminder that critical judgments are supported with analysis and interpretation.

1 The Need to Think Critically About Communication

Though communication is certainly a tool for conducting the everyday business of our lives, it is also at the core of who we are, what we think, and what we do. The debate over whether communication reflects or creates the reality we call our lives oversimplifies the relationship between communication and the things about which we communicate. It does not make sense to say media stories about the O. J. Simpson trial create the meaning of the trial, or that the trial has some fundamental truth or meaning that gets reflected in the media. Our communication reflects the world within and around us, and simultaneously creates it. For now, "symbols shape meaning" is a phrase that best captures the idea that communication gives meaning to reality, whether reality is an object in the physical world or an idea in our minds. Imagining the meaning of any pre-existing thing or thought in this world, untouched by communication, is difficult. Because most of this book presents a vocabulary for critically unraveling the many shades of meaning, this chapter explains why we should go through the trouble of learning to think critically about communication. In short, communication plays a significant role in who we are, what we know, and what we do.

Who We Are

Communication shapes our identities. At an interpersonal level, how others interact with us shapes the images we have of ourselves. Even the most amateur psychologist believes that children we criticize and never praise will grow up with little confidence in their own abilities. Parents and teachers share their potential to influence children with books, television programs, computer games, advertisements, speeches, news reports, films, and rituals. Public communication, in particular, legitimizes ways of being.

Hailing and Individual Identities

We create and recreate our self-concepts in childhood stories, rituals of adolescence, music, films, museums, speeches, movie stars, and fashion. The princess, the rebel, the bachelor, the intellectual, the patriot, the flirt, the buffoon, the middle class, the immigrant, the childless are who we may be. "Super mom" emerged in the 1980s and legitimized ways of being a woman. Super mom, a woman who works outside the home and maintains primary responsibility for the house and children, is now a familiar character in the media, at home, and at the office. As super mom continued to reveal herself in magazine advertisements, television shows, films, and conversations, we assumed her presence as a natural fact of life. "Soccer moms" were distinguished as a target audience in the 1996 presidential campaign. Soccer moms are affluent, suburban, super moms. They were characterized politically as unwilling to take policy risks, favoring federal programs designed as safety nets, and especially interested in issues relating to the family.

Stuart Hall (1985), a scholar working within the interdisciplinary field of Cultural Studies, explains that we enact identities in the ways we address one another. *Hailing* is the name Hall gives to this process of imposing identities through address, whether verbal or visual, interpersonal or public.[1] Hall describes a form of hailing prominent when he was growing up in Jamaica and its influence on his sense of himself:

> I was constantly hailed a "coloured." The way the term was articulated with other terms in the syntaxes of race and ethnicity was such as to produce the meaning, in effect: "not black." The "blacks" were the rest—the vast majority of the people, the ordinary folk. To be "coloured" was to belong to the "mixed" ranks of the brown middle class, a cut above the rest—an inspiration if not in reality. My family attached great weight to these finely graded classificatory distinctions and, because of what it signified in terms of distinctions of class, status, race, color, insisted on the inscription. (p. 108)

Hailing puts boundaries around who we may become. Young women, in the recent past, were rarely hailed as providers or professionals. Today, women are hailed as providers and homemakers, that is, "super moms" and "soccer moms." Whereas it is easy to blame the media for presenting stereotypes, we personally, albeit unconsciously, limit the potential identities of others in the ways we hail them. For instance, you may hail your friend as someone who is athletic, fashionable, and knowledgeable about politics. When, however, you have a business problem, you never turn to this friend. Married couples with children may come to hail one another as mother and father more than as lovers. Our parents may always hail us as children. We are all guilty of settling into a limited number of ways of hailing those we know and care about most. In the following passage, William Raspberry (1991), a journalist for the *Washington Post*, illustrates how hailing influences actual identities:

> Black youngsters in the inner cities are moved by the myth that blacks have special athletic gifts, particularly with regard to basketball. Asian youngsters are influenced by the myth that they have special gifts for math and science. Jewish youngsters accept the myth that their group has a special gift for the power of the written word.
>
> Now all these myths are, by themselves, worthless. But when they evoke a sense of identity and the energy to move ahead, something happens. People work at the things they believe they are innately capable of achieving. So it is not uncommon to see a black kid working up to bedtime, practicing his double pump scoop, his behind the back dribble, his left-handed jumpshot. And after a few months of work, if he has any athletic talent at all, he proves the myth. (p. 88)

Although we often develop beyond the confines of socially determined identities, we will typically define ourselves in relation to them. Betty Friedan (1981), the well known feminist writer, reveals the double bind that those who fight against socially accepted identities may find themselves in when she says that women who continue reacting against that male-defined social structure will continue to be "defined and limited by its terms" (p. 40). In other words, to reject a socially constructed identity is, to some degree, to accept it. For instance, the following assertions reinforce the legitimacy of stereotypes: "I am Jewish but I do not support the policies of the Israeli prime minister." "I am a woman but I am really good at reading maps." "Even though I am Asian, I do not understand computers."

One cannot avoid the impact of communication on his or her identity. Being ignored can even be thought of as a form of hailing that constructs an identity that is insignificant or illegitimate. From the statue of the Virgin Mary and Jesus in front of the courthouse to the holiday greeting cards found in most stores, nonChristian religions are relegated to the margins of American society. Gay and bisexual individuals undergo a systematic marginalization of their sexual identities because they are, from the time they are babies, hailed as heterosexuals: "When will you get married and have children?" "Do you have a boyfriend/girlfriend yet?" "He is, you know, 'funny,' 'not right'." In the words of lesbian activist Jill Johnston (1973), "Identity is what you can say you are according to what they say you can be" (p. 68).

Hailing and Cultural Identities

The foregoing discussion reveals that communication shapes identities that are larger than the individual. Communication, in fact, creates, reflects, and maintains cultures within our society. Clifford Geertz (1973), a well-known cultural anthropologist, links culture and communication in his definition of culture as "an historically transmitted pattern of meanings embodied in symbols, a system of inherited conceptions expressed in symbolic form by means of which men [sic] communicate, perpetuate and develop their knowledge about and attitudes towards life" (p. 89). John Fiske (1989), a scholar of popular culture, summarizes culture as meaning and the making of meaning: "Culture is the constant process of producing meaning of and from our social experience, and such meanings necessarily produce a social identity for the people" (p. 1). Communication and culture are inseparable.

We are all a part of several overlapping cultures, including race, ethnicity, religion, nationality, and social class. Cultures form in shared codes of meaning that range from formal and conscious systems of religious beliefs to informal and less conscious myths of a generational culture. A religious culture infuses words, actions, people, events, days of the year, and artifacts with meaning. Similarly, generational groups establish and maintain their attitudes, beliefs, and values in their choice of heroes, music, and style of dress. A few friends who meet regularly and establish a secret handshake probably do not constitute a culture. It is difficult, if not impossible, to determine when such a group becomes a culture. Friendship circles, classrooms, and the workplace can be viewed, however, as cultures insofar as the people and their symbols come together in *systems of meaning* that shape their identity.

A system of meaning is a world view, a way of thinking, a pattern of thought, or a set of interrelated ideas. Most obviously, religions establish systems of thought or meaning: God created the universe; God established that people are morally responsible for their actions; immoral actions are sins against God and will be punished in this life and in the hereafter. A generation of individuals may also share a system of meaning: Democracy is the best form of government; communist governments are the enemy of democracy; people who live in communist governments are unhappy; democratic ends justify any means of maintaining democracy. Professions are cultures when professional associations, meetings, newsletters, dress and behavioral codes pass along the standards that identify the professional. Typically, such shared systems of meaning and forms of expression develop over time.

Overlapping and Contradictory Identities

Because we are all a part of many cultures simultaneously, we have complex and often contradictory identities. Once upon a time, experts in personal development agreed that psychologically healthy individuals acquired a unified and consistent identity. The theory of a singular identity is exemplified in Somerset Maugham's drama, *The Razor's Edge* (1944), in which the main character travels to Asia in order to "find himself." Today, we have lost confidence in this theory as we acknowledge, and even celebrate, our overlapping identities. For instance, many Americans describe themselves in terms of a "hyphenated-ethnicity," such as, Greek-American, Serbian-American, or Polish-American, in an attempt to preserve their cultural history. Women's liberation groups have splintered into subcultures of women, including African American, working class, Christian, lesbian women, or some combination of these groups.

Often our cultural identities will come into conflict with one another. A young woman born and reared in New York City by her Syrian parents may hold opposite beliefs about dating as a result of her identity as a Syrian and as an American. In her autobiographical work, *Alchemy of Race and Rights* (1991), Patricia Williams, an African American female lawyer and professor of legal studies, unpacks the contradictions among her professional, racial, and gender identities. The following excerpt from this work touches on a few of the contradictions that were brought to Ms. Williams's attention in the ways others hailed her.

> I heard the same-different words addressed to me, a perceived white-male-socialized black woman. . . . Such acknowledgement complicates the supposed purity of gender, race, voice, boundary; it allows us to acknowledge the utility of such categorizations for certain purposes and the necessity of their breakdown on other occasions. (p. 10)

Just as we struggle individually with contradictory identities, cultures struggle for dominance in the public realm. Some of the more obvious players in cultural power struggles are age, race, ethnicity, sex/gender, and social class. A group gains power in the cultural realm when its meanings and ways of making meaning are assumed to be natural by the most people. Economic and cultural power are not unrelated, for they fuel one another. Cultures become dominant when powerful agents of socialization, such as media, government, and education, assume their view of the world and hail all others according to that view.

For instance, Patricia Williams has to master the codes and conventions of the white-male culture in order to function successfully in her profession. In so doing, she may assume so much of the dominant culture that she can no longer be certain of the seams of her identities. Some people might even say that she has been "co-opted" by the dominant culture. A dominant culture co-opts by allowing a competing culture to participate in the public meaning process while it controls the scripts. In the condition of co-optation, African American women lawyers would think and act in ways that favor the dominant culture at their own expense.

If there is a dominant culture in the United States, it is believed to be the culture of Western European, Protestant, white men. However, the presence of one, unified, dominant culture doing battle with minority cultures is an exaggerated notion. There are few individuals whose entire being fits into dominant cultural categories. At some time in their lives, almost every person identifies with marginal cultures. An apparently "dominant" male may be marginalized at school because of his cultural neighborhood or at work because of his generational culture. Not all people experience systematic, institutional, economic oppression, but most of us experience more and less power within our own cultural identities.

Furthermore, the notion of "a dominant culture" assumes a singular identity of consolidated economic resources and cultural leanings. Maintaining dominance over cultural meanings is an ongoing and difficult campaign, because numerous cultures compete for their systems of meaning and forms of expression to become the norm. People have some choice and therefore power over their cultural meanings. If there is a dominant culture, it is a process that never rests.

Patricia Williams illustrates the difficulty of absolute cultural tyranny: She may accommodate or assimilate a white, male, Western European identity but she has many identities that become more or less relevant in her daily life. Some of these identities may challenge the so-called "dominant" way of life, as they do in her *Alchemy of Race and Rights.* As minorities gain rights, they find the power to challenge the dominant meanings and the cultures that control them.

Though I have been emphasizing the possibility of cultural democracy in which we openly and fairly wrestle for control of meanings, I do not dismiss the dominance of white, often ethnically ambiguous, Protestant, middle-class men in the United States. It has been mostly their views of law, film, education, art, intelligence, marriage, and so on, that have established the norms in this country. I believe exceptions are possible. I would like to believe there are challenges to the so-called "dominant view of the world."

In summary, our personal identities are inseparable from our cultural identities, and both are inseparable from communication. Communication of all kinds shapes identities and maintains them through shared systems of meaning and forms of expression. According to this view, "being"—who you are—entwines with "knowing"—what you think. I now turn to the topic of *knowing,* to address the significant role of communication in human thought.

What We Know

We know about the way it was before we were born through the stories of "old timers," museums, textbooks, films, television, paintings, music, and literature. Knowing, similar to being, is shaped through communication. We often use the words *facts, beliefs,* and *ideas* to describe what we know. I will clarify these terms, and others associated with our thought processes, while discussing the relationship among communication, perceptual knowledge, and conceptual knowledge.

Perceptual Knowing

Perception is a logical starting point to develop the claim that knowledge is rooted in communication, because sensory impressions—that is, seeing, hearing, touching, smelling, and tasting—are often considered to be the most basic, experiential, objective, and factual aspects of knowledge. Perceptual knowledge is often wrongly assumed to be pure because it is free of subjective influences. We say, "I saw it with my own eyes" to convince others we speak the absolute truth. However, it is rare, if not impossible, to perceive "naked" facts. We selectively attend and present perceptual experiences influenced by an entire history of communication. For instance, once we learn a new word, we may encounter the word frequently. It is quite likely we previously encountered, but not consciously perceived, the word.

Words, and other symbols, aid and direct our perceptions and vice versa. Cultures may not even have words for objects and events that are deemed insignificant or go unrecognized. Recent debate over the nature of "sexual harassment" illustrates the close relationship between what we say and what we see. The term was not in common use twenty years ago, although certainly events that are today perceived as "sexually harassing" took place 20 years ago. The evolving meaning of sexual harassment is also an example of how a cultural group, in this case a culture of women, attempts to gain power by having its meanings accepted as the norm. The struggle over the meaning of sexual harassment continues, but the struggle itself suggests American culture is perceiving events that were not noticed 20 years ago, perceived differently, and/or deemed insignificant.

Even scientists, dedicated to the objective discovery of knowledge, see the world selectively. Consider that symptoms of the AIDS virus (HIV) appeared and went unnoticed in 1978. By 1981, 159 official cases were registered and rumors about the disease were spreading throughout the gay community. The disease was not, however, officially named until 1982, or publicly-politically recognized until it was evident in the white, heterosexual population (Grmek, 1990). Obviously, the virus was a fact, but it was one that our interests, beliefs, and values—reinforced through daily communication—did not encourage us to see.

Historical facts are similarly determined by the subjectivities of the storytellers. Archeological ruins, artifacts, and radiocarbon dating of organic substances established that Bantu-Africans developed Great Zimbabwe, a medieval city of stone. The colonial governments that later established themselves in Africa recreated the facts into a story that Great Zimbabwe was built by pre-Christian Greeks or Egyptians. Since the independence of Zimbabwe from British-Rhodesian rule, the facts are being reformulated (Garlake, 1982).

The same sort of selective perception applies to news reporters who investigate the events of the day and selectively present them to the public. There is potentially an infinite number of reportable events, more by far than can be reported by news agencies. An example that again illustrates the power that some women have gained in recent decades is the rise of media coverage on issues of middle-aged pregnancies and child day care. Such stories are not coincidentally related to the rise of women in newsrooms. Though these issues are significant to 30- and 40-year-old professionals, there are important events and issues that they never witness because they are limited, as are all people, by their particular cultural visions of how the world is.

Conceptual Knowing

Insofar as we can separate stages of thought, conceptions follow perceptions in that they are more abstract. Whereas perceptions are concrete, sensory, and considered factual, conceptions take us into the realm of ideas. I perceive the boy running down the street. I conceive that he is in danger. Often considered to be informed by facts, conceptions include beliefs, attitudes, and values. Beliefs refer to ideas about existence and truth: I believe that many people who commit crimes are driven by economic poverty. Attitudes refer to feelings of acceptance or rejection: I reject poverty as an excuse for a crime. Values refer to the relative importance we assign to facts, beliefs, and attitudes: I value safety.

In most situations, however, perceptions cannot be separated from conceptions, and beliefs, attitudes, and values cannot be separated from one another. Seventeenth and eighteenth century philosophers theorized that the human mind contained separate entities, called "faculties," that could operate independently. In such a scenario, one part of the mind could perceive information, another part would reason from the information, and still another part was responsible for emotions. Today, we accept the idea that the mind-brain operates holistically, so that perceiving the boy, believing and fearing that he is in danger, and valuing safety are simultaneous acts. The fusion of facts and ideas, or perceptions and conceptions, accounts for our ignorance about "the facts" of AIDS. They became inseparable from beliefs that homosexuality does not exist, or that it is rare, perverse, immoral, and perhaps punishable by death.

Ideological Knowing

When ideas show up together in patterns or systems that reinforce one another, as do the previous ideas about homosexuality and AIDS, they are called *ideologies*. Ideologies are powerful because they become the unquestioned basis for so much of our thought and action. Ideologies common in American thought include the following:

> *An Ideology of Super Mom:* Women who live up to their potential should raise children, maintain a household, and "enjoy" a full-time career.
>
> *An Ideology of Crime:* Most people who commit crimes come from disadvantaged family backgrounds. If we can fix families, we can fix crime.
>
> *An Ideology of Heterosexuality:* Human beings were put on this earth to procreate. Everyone should marry a member of the opposite sex, procreate, and raise their children together.
>
> *An Ideology of God:* God exists. God sets out the moral laws that humans should follow. God punishes immoral behavior in this life and in the hereafter.

Talking about the power of ideologies without introducing Karl Marx's ideas on the subject is difficult.[2] Marx, and many who follow his philosophy, assert that a dominant culture produces ideological thinking (for Marx, it is the culture of capitalism) to economically undermine competing cultures. The ideology of work, often referred to as the Protestant Ethic, benefits the wealthy over the poor and middle classes by encouraging the latter to work hard for the financial gain of the former. Those who believe in the ideology will work hard because they believe it is what good people do and because they will be economically rewarded for their goodness. If they never rise above meager financial rewards, the ideology directs them to blame their inherent lack of goodness rather than the economic policies of the upper classes. Thus, in the traditional Marxist view, ideologies translate into money. The ideology of work brings money to a few at the expense of many. The ideology of super mom limits women's economic independence by ostensibly encouraging women to develop careers in the public arena but maintain their full-time role as wives and mothers.

Today, a succession of Marxist thinkers have broadened Marx's view of ideology beyond economic oppression.[3] The ideology of heterosexuality, for instance, oppresses gays by hailing them as social deviants. The ideology of heterosexuality actually infringes on the well-being of all individuals who choose not to marry or bear children. Even couples who are physically unable to bear children become less valuable than procreating couples. Similarly, religious ideologies have historically been used to oppress people. People who are socially oppressed are often denied political and economic power. Beyond traditional Marxism, we are concerned with this wider range of ideological effects.

Another difference between traditional Marxism and most Marxist thinkers today is that the latter believe all cultures have ideologies. Ideologies, in fact, are a defining feature of a culture. Recall that cultures are established and maintained by systems of meaning and ways of expressing those meanings. Ideologies are recurrent systems of meaning. Americans have ideologies, as do catholics, westerners, democrats, baby boomers, pharmacists, gays, and feminists. Hailing is a concept that explains the link between ideologies and identities. When a person accepts being hailed in a particular way, they tacitly accept a worldview. For instance, an adult hails a child, the child answers, a conversation ensues. The act of participating in the conversation incorporates ideologies into our social systems. In this case, the ideology re-establishes the child as powerless, innocent, and nonsexual. The adult is all-knowing and all-powerful. The process by which communication positions people in ideologies is referred to as "interpellation" (Althusser, 1971; Belsey, 1980; Fiske, 1987). Hailing and interpellation are different phases of the same process. Hailing calls forth an identity; interpellation is the entire system of social identities and beliefs that give that identity meaning.

Ideological thinking has its advantages in that it often unconsciously guides thinking and behavior. Ideologies provide people with commonplaces that make communication possible. Basically, ideologies make communication, and life, a little easier than if we had to reinvent the wheel every time we wanted to use it.

Not necessarily false, unethical, or even unavoidable, ideologies do close off our options. The ease of ideologies is their downfall for they quell the need to talk about many things. We assume agreement. In this way all ideologies, regardless of the culture that produces them, suppress thought and action. We have discussed thought. Let us now turn to action.

What We Do

Our actions are an extension of who we are and what we know. As the columnist William Raspberry (1991) pointed out, hailing blacks as naturally athletic makes it "not uncommon to see a black kid working up to bedtime, practicing his double-pump scoop, his behind the back dribble, his left-handed jump shot (p. 88)." Children proudly hailed as "go-getters" may strive to achieve more goals than children hailed in less glowing ways. The super mom image encourages women to develop themselves professionally while raising a family. Our cultural identities influence the foods we eat, the occasions we celebrate, and the ways we spend our leisure. National cultures create social policies and wage war. Knowledge of past wars will shape our strategies in today's wars. We avoid traveling alone at night because of the bombardment of violence on television news. Ideologies of heterosexuality lead us to marriage, as well as to question those who do not marry.

In summary, our lives consist of who we are, what we think, and what we do. And none of these things exists apart from meaningful communication. The remaining pages of this book will argue that thinking critically about communication allows one to intervene in the process of meaning and thereby actively influence the meanings in, and perhaps of, our lives.

Notes

1. Hall borrowed and developed the concept of hailing from Althusser.

2. Marx's economic theory is laid out in Marx (1961); The role of culture in economics is the subject of Marx and Engels (1973).

3. Althusser's (1971) rendering of Marx has had considerable impact on contemporary Marxist thinking. For an overview of contemporary Marxism in critical studies, see Belsey (1980); Eagleton (1976); Fiske (1987); Hall (1985); and White (1987).

2 How to Think Critically About Communication

Communication has power over us when we believe our identities and ideas are absolute and essential. We have power over communication, and much of our lives, when we critically question the naturalness of our meanings. We can, for instance, transform fear of an enemy into respect. We can redefine youth and beauty. We can change our beliefs and behaviors regarding cigarettes, food, and alcohol. We do have control over our lives because we have control over the meanings we give to our images and words. Communication criticism is a way of taking control that academics have developed. In this chapter, I will overview three phases of thought that make up a formal and systematic process of critical thinking: analysis, interpretation, and evaluation. We should keep in mind that critical thought rarely proceeds in such linear and distinct stages. Nevertheless, this formal model is useful for identifying the essential qualities of critical thinking. And though formal criticism is unlikely to be our life's work, a slow walk through the process can only improve the ongoing casual criticism that we engage in on an everyday basis.

Critical Evaluation

When we think critically about communication, we ultimately make judgments. Judging, or evaluating, communication is most familiar to us.

It is, therefore, a good place to begin this profile of how to think critically. Judging communication is also the one aspect of critical thinking most obviously linked to the goals of this book, to gain power over the meanings we make. Although it is considered the final phase of systematic critical thought, evaluation often pushes critical thinking forward. For these reasons, I will address evaluation before analysis and interpretation.

Evaluating communication is common and serves some very practical individual and social needs. When we engage in a formal talk, interview, or informal argument, we typically evaluate the effectiveness of our communication. We may evaluate the potential effects of a film before we invite our young nephew to join us. We also find it necessary to judge the truth of communication numerous times in any given day. Is my friend lying to me? Does this film portray a true story? Is the computer salesperson exaggerating about the computer's potential? Is the television news report accurate? When we question the news reporter's, our friend's, or the salesperson's motives, methods of investigation and presentation, we are also evaluating their ethics of communication. Standards of truth and ethics are necessary to social order because they allow us to assume that most human communication is sincere. Without the assumption of sincerity, we could not successfully engage in the most basic communicative act.

These familiar judgments *can* lead us into making some conscious choices about our identities, ideas, and behaviors. The italicized *can* is significant because of the difference between judging communication and judging communication as part of a critical process. So far, we have only illustrated the former. Judgment becomes critical when we can explain how and why symbols and people come together in ways that effectively, truthfully, or ethically shape meaning. Understanding why particular communicative acts work, or do not work, makes us better speakers and listeners. It allows us to choose when to influence and when to be influenced. Thinking critically about the effects, truth, and ethics of communication protects us from fraud. It also encourages us to reconsider the beliefs and ideologies in which we are interpellated. It is the ongoing process of critical thinking, not judgment alone, that allows us the power of choice. Evaluation leads to critical thinking when we turn our judgments into questions: Why is the film effective? In what ways is the speech truthful and ethical? How does contemporary rock music shape our identities and actions? Answering these questions requires analysis and interpretation.

Critical Analysis

If we are to critically evaluate meaningful communication, we need to know how it is made. The process of analysis breaks communication into its essential parts. The essential parts of communication include the specific communication text or texts to be interpreted and judged, and the context(s) surrounding the text(s). Analysis describes communication more than it interprets how meaning is made. It sets up the case for critical interpretation and evaluation. When done thoroughly, analysis prods and directs critical thinking. For this reason, the analysis of a communication text and context can be useful as a first step in critical thinking. Whether or not a critic starts here, there must be some boundaries put around the communication text and context.

Analyzing the Communication Text

The communication text is a very specific set of symbols exchanged among people. The text may be a conversation, a book, an advertisement, a newspaper article, a speech, the lyrics of a song, or a dialogue of a film or television program. Beyond these verbal texts, we can think critically about visual images, behavioral rituals, aural symbols such as music, or actual objects that have communicative value. The chapter on language provides a better sense of all the things that have communicative potential. For now, it is important to draw boundaries around the object of your thought.

For instance, one may examine a Presidential State of the Union Address, a television advertisement for Pepsi, or an entire Pepsi television ad campaign. Several things are important to keep in mind as we select a text or texts for analysis. First, it is essential that one have an accurate copy (video, film, and/or transcript) of the text itself. Though we can engage in some critical thinking about a film we saw last week, formal criticism requires that the critic read, listen to, and/or watch the text(s) often. Because formal criticism is quite exhausting when done thoroughly, it often makes sense to select a portion of a longer text, such as a scene or sequence of a film.

Not all communication is equally worthy of critical thought. Currently, there is substantial controversy over what texts are worthy of reflective study.[1] As communication critics, however, we are not only concerned with what the intellectual elite call the "great works" but with any communication that shapes the ideas and identities of people. Thus, a television special on the O.J. Simpson trial may be significant because it influences the public's beliefs about race, crime, sports, abusive relationships, and/or the legal process. Because communication also reflects ideas and identities, the value of a text may rest in what it can tell us about a culture. Cookbooks for instance, provide some insight into the people who use them. Recipe books written in the American West in the late 1800s contain formulas for perfume, hair growth, cleaning potions, and a wide range of substitute cooking ingredients, as so many were difficult to come by. Cookbooks from the 1950s and 1960s include lengthy discussions on kitchen appliances, decorating food and table, and how to please one's husband. In any case, the critic should ask her- or himself, "So what?" early in the critical process. The answer does not have to change the world but simply increase our understanding of people, including ourselves.

Analyzing the Communication Context

A text does not have meaning without a context. A joke told by, and to, a man may have a different meaning if the same joke is told by a woman, to women. Unraveling the meaning of a text, therefore, requires an analysis of the communication context. Scholars have cast the communication context in many ways ranging from the basic sender-message—channel—receiver models to social models that identify the institutions that produce and control meaning. Certainly, all contexts may become more or less relevant to meaning. Most critical thinkers prefer some models over others. Here I will summarize three models useful in guiding a critical analysis of the communication context: The **rhetorical situation** is a model introduced by Lloyd Bitzer (1968) and developed primarily in the field of speech communication; **supertext** is a way of looking at context that has been developed by scholars working within the interdisciplinary domain called cultural studies (Fiske, 1987; Grossberg, 1987; Morley, 1989); and the notion of a **discursive formation** is a model for communication contexts developed by Michel Foucault (1972), a critical social theorist. The critic should consider the communication text as it is situated in one, or all, of these models.

Context as a Rhetorical Situation

The rhetorical situation is a model that was developed for studying purposeful communication. Most political and legal speeches intend to persuade a specific audience, as do advertisements and any kind of sales pitch. Informative communication is goal-oriented as well, for the newsperson and the teacher aim to impart information to their audiences. Purposeful communication has three parts that the critic must consider: **exigency, audience,** and **constraints.**

Rhetorical situations form around urgencies, also called *exigencies,* that can be settled through communication. Exigencies abound: Saddam Hussein created an exigency when he sent Iraqi troops into Kuwait; the cost of health care is an exigency; misbehaving children are an exigency; corporate "downsizing" is an exigency. Social exigencies, such as the need to reduce crime, educate the public about AIDS, or mourn the death of a leader, invite people to become part of a public dialogue. The resulting communication, whether it be speeches, documentary films, television shows, music, or funeral rituals, aims to relieve the exigency.

The next step in analyzing a rhetorical situation is to describe the **audience(s)** with the potential to resolve the exigencies. The critic must always consider a particular audience because different audiences construct different meanings. For example, when Pat Buchanan spoke at the Republican National Convention in Houston, Texas in August of 1992, he had many exigencies, including pressure from the Republican party to throw his support(ers) behind presidential nominee George Bush. Buchanan, a leader for the more conservative Republicans and a previous competitor for the presidential nomination, aimed to overcome party divisions in favor of a unified backing for Bush. Buchanan's audience included his supporters for presidency but also anyone who could be moved to vote for Bush in the election and thereby resolve the problem. Buchanan's *immediate* audience included the Republicans attending the convention and his speech. His immediate audience, and the general American public who tuned into the speech via television, made up Buchanan's *actual* audience. Finally, the critic may consider Buchanan's *ideal* audience; that is, those who agreed with the policies he had promoted on the campaign trail, and who would be most receptive to his message.

The critic must go beyond naming the audience to characterizing the attitudes, beliefs, values, experiences, interests, needs, and knowledge that may be relevant to its understanding of the speech. Buchanan's ideal audience, for instance, was very concerned with the topic of gay rights. Several cities and states around the country were proposing legislation to guarantee gays equal protection under the law. The Democrats, led by Bill Clinton, were proposing to lift the military ban on homosexuals. A major theme in Buchanan's campaign was to stop such legislation. His ideal audience believed such laws offer special rights to gays. It also believed that homosexuality is immoral and in conflict with family values, another major theme of the campaign. Buchanan's ideal audience opposed legalized abortions and favored voluntary prayer in public schools.

These qualities of an audience make up its "psychographic" profile. The critic may generate a psychographic profile by consulting opinion polls found in campaign headquarters, newspapers, or marketing journals. More often the critic may have access to a demographic profile of the audience, which includes the sociocultural categories that the audience members belong to: sexual identity, sexual orientation, religion, ethnicity, race, profession, educational level, income level, age, and political affiliation, to mention a few. The demographic profile will suggest a psychographic profile. Generalizing about the audience is necessary to communication and the criticism of communication. There are always individual differences and variations from the norm, but most public messages are designed to make sense to the largest possible audience, and they do. Even though Americans, for instance, may identify with very different cultural groups, they are exposed to many of the same messages via school, parents, and media, and therefore develop many of the same codes for making sense of messages. Millions of people can watch and make similar sense of the same movie. That is not to say that all viewers will construct meanings that are exactly the same, but their understandings would not be so divergent that some of them think the movie is about space aliens and others view it as a story about animal life in the Sahara Desert.

The critic extends a sketch of the rhetorical situation by thinking about all of the factors that can impede or aid the effectiveness of the message. These factors, called **constraints,** include just about anything—the weather, social issues, attitudes, beliefs, and past events—that may influence the speaker's abilities, the audience's reception of the speaker's message, or both. To complete our analysis of Buchanan's rhetorical situation, we must examine the forces that helped him find and foil support for George Bush.

Some of the factors that worked in Buchanan's favor include the following:

- He spoke on the first day of the convention—on the same day as Ronald Reagan, who generated a lot of attention.
- Buchanan's presentation on the opening day also suggested the Republican party was supportive of his efforts.
- In the months previous to the convention he had the support of Rush Limbaugh, the popular, conservative, radio talk show host.
- He was very well-known as he had been a presidential nominee in the election.
- Many supporters were, similar to Buchanan, actively opposed to gay rights.

Some of the factors that may have hampered his efforts to gain support for Bush:

- The accusation of insincerity, given that he had insulted Bush throughout the duration of his own campaign.
- The loyalty of his own followers, who might not want to give up the fight and support Bush.
- Buchanan's position against gay rights, and support from the controversial Rush Limbaugh, which offended many people.

I mention this last constraint as working for and against Buchanan as a reminder of the complexity of the rhetorical context. Though the rhetorical situation divides the communication context into exigencies, audiences, and constraints, there is considerable overlap among these categories.

Context as Supertext

Bitzer's rhetorical situation has been criticized for separating communication from its context.[2] In other words, it seems to suggest that there is a communication situation and then there is communication. Critics often find the best profile of the communication context is communication itself. **Supertext** is a concept that casts rhetorical situations as they are created in communication. Supertext is a sublevel of communication texts that, according to Fiske (1987), "provide [the critic with] evidence of the ways that the various meanings of the primary text are activated and inserted into the culture for various audiences or subcultures" (p. 285). The supertext of Buchanan's convention speech would include all of the communication that becomes relevant to how audiences make sense of the speech.

The supertext includes the history of communication that shapes the rhetorical situation. A culture's communication history often reveals "communication genres," which are recurring situations and communication strategies for addressing the situations. For instance, Buchanan's speech and the rhetorical situation it encompasses fall into the genre of American convention speeches. According to Campbell and Jamieson (1976), a critic pursuing the generic context of a communication text "seeks to recreate the symbolic context in which the act emerged" (p. 27). In so doing, critics learn communication is shaped by prior communication.

Beyond the genre that shapes a text and context, supertext includes the texts that precede and follow the text and become relevant to its meaning. Supertext includes all of the news stories, talk radio, promotional advertisements, political cartoons, and even speech critics that influenced how different audiences came to make sense of Buchanan's words. If the press had not called attention to Buchanan's gay "bashing," it would have had a less significant role, or a different role, in the meaning of the speech. In fact, if you were to hear Buchanan speak tomorrow, this very discussion of Buchanan's speech would become part of the supertext for your understanding of the speech. Thus, supertext is not a fixed concept but an ever-changing one. The idea that a text is actually part of past and future texts makes the boundaries of any communication text problematic.

In sum, when rhetorical situations are constructed through supertexts, the critic views exigencies, audience, and constraints as part of the reality that is shaped by communication. The speeches of a religious cult leader present an interesting example of rhetorical situations as supertexts. A question for critical consideration is, how do these speeches persuade people to give up family, wealth, and ultimately life for their beliefs? The rhetorical situation directs us to analyze the audience, exigencies, and constraints to which the speech addresses itself. Supertext directs us to analyze the situation through the speeches themselves and through the other speeches, doctrines, conversations, letters, magazines, and rituals of the cult members. Supertext reminds us that audiences are histories of communication.

Context as a Discursive Formation

A **discursive formation** attempts to capture what is called the "epistemological" context of a communicative event. Epistemology is the study of what people at any given time in history consider to be truth and knowledge and how that truth and knowledge is created or becomes known. For instance, the dominant epistemology of the Middle Ages was faith in God. The Church played a major role in legitimizing topics of discussion and determining what was truthful. In the period of Enlightenment, scientific ways of generating knowledge prevailed. Michel Foucault is responsible for developing the idea of a discursive formation as a system of communication rules that govern the nature of knowledge— actually the sociology of knowledge—in a given time.

People's beliefs, attitudes, and values have an epistemological context and, therefore, all communication can be positioned in a discursive formation. The discursive formation that shapes talk about death, for instance, includes the relations among the social systems that control thought and communication about death. These social systems include the publishing industry, education, funeral directors, religions, and medical doctors. The systems are governed by three categories of rules that determine what can be discussed, who may discuss it, and how it must be discussed (Foucault 1972, Chaps. 3 and 4).

To illustrate the critical analysis of a discursive formation, let us consider how Buchanan's speech at the National Republican Convention was governed by rules of communication. The three governing rules outlined above shape the Convention in general. Some topics are open (and expected to be addressed) for discussion at political conventions; others are silenced. The National Convention, for instance, is not the place to discuss differences among party members or to hammer out specific political policies. Some individuals and institutions have authority over others to speak about specific subject matters. Past leaders of the political party, for instance, are given great respect. Often the stories of common people will be told and their lessons heeded. Finally, there are enunciative rules that govern the way individuals may use language, reason, organize, and present their ideas. Not only do we expect a strong degree of formality in an address to a national political convention but we expect the speaker to follow the formula of nomination speeches.

So far, we have discussed governing rules in a general way. These same three governing rules—what can be talked about, who can talk about it, and how they must talk about it—can also be applied to specific topics addressed within Buchanan's speech. For instance, Buchanan's talk about abortion is constrained. Our culture limits the topics within abortion; we select our own authorities on the subject, and we dictate appropriate language. Clearly a discursive formation is so immense that it is impossible to fully know one without dedicating one's life to its discovery. Nevertheless, the idea that communication is shaped over time by a variety of institutions and ways of talking is significant to a critic.

Even a cursory consideration of a discursive formation aids critical thinking in two important ways. First, Foucault's governing rules help critics reveal the many people, ideas, and forms of expression that are, at any given time, outside the discursive formation. For example, children are systematically excluded from most decision making. People who do not have medical degrees are, in American society, excluded from legitimate discussions about illness. Though the idea of hearing from everyone sounds abstract and ideal, we do need fresh ideas to solve persistent social and personal problems. Second, consideration of the governing rules that determine communication provides a simple reminder that meaning and the making of meaning are often arbitrary, oppressive, and open to change. The emphasis Foucault puts on social institutions makes discursive formations the broadest form of analyzing the communication context but it is not incompatible with rhetorical situations and supertexts.

In summary, if you want to understand how communication works, you must study more than a particular communication text. Any communication text—a conversation between two friends, a film, or political speech—comes to make sense in a particular context. Thinking critically about communication is a systematic process that requires an analysis of the communication text and its context. Obviously, formal criticism requires one to do some research to fully understand the communication text, its creators, its audience, the supertext and its discursive formations.

■■■■   Critical Interpretation

Interpretation is the phase of critical thinking that concentrates on *how* and/or *why* messages come to mean what they do. We interpret, for instance, when we understand that the black youth pictured in the ad for athletic shoes provides the shoes with credibility because its audience believes blacks are good at sports. This interpretative statement clearly includes some analysis of the advertisement's context. We know who the target audience is and its beliefs about African Americans and sports. What is less obvious in interpretive thinking, is it depends on our knowing some basic principles of communication. The interpretation of the advertisement for athletic shoes employs principles regarding the role of beliefs and credibility in meaning.

The critical thinker uses principles or theories of communication to answer the interpretive "how" and/or "why" symbols come to mean certain things to people. Communication theories, that is, generalizations about the workings of communication, are abundant. They are developed in a variety of fields, including philosophy, anthropology, literature, psychology, and film studies. Every theory frames communication in a particular way, emphasizing some parts of the exchange over others. Theoretical frameworks are similar to eyeglasses that can produce different visions of the same object. Many theories can be useful guides through critical interpretation, depending on the interests, goals, and assumptions of the critical thinker.

The remaining chapters of this book present theoretical concepts that should encourage different visions or interpretations of communication. The concepts presented are in no way exhaustive, but they do embody the fundamental principles of communication and how these principles have been, and can be, adapted to thinking critically about most communication. The fundamental principles of communication may be found in the ancient study of persuasive speaking, which here are synthesized with more contemporary-critical approaches to popular culture.

Critical Concepts Rooted in
the Practical Art of Rhetoric

Greek and Roman writers, and speakers in Antiquity, developed a systematic theory of communication, called *rhetoric*.[3] Twenty-five hundred years ago, the study of rhetoric emphasized the practice of speaking to the public. The citizens of democratic Athens regularly gathered in the courts and town squares to speak about legal and policy issues (Agard, 1960). Public speaking was the primary means of shaping public opinion and therefore essential to the entire democratic decision-making process. Policy making and legal decisions were believed to involve a special kind of thinking based on public opinion and probability. The most feasible military action or taxation policy cannot be determined with certainty and so people must persuade one another to agree with their opinions. It is through rhetoric, or persuasive communication, that publics form and effect social action. It was in this context that schools of rhetoric developed to educate the democratic citizenry.

Classical theories of rhetoric emphasize purposeful speech, and how the effective speaker will adapt his or her ideas, structure, language, and presentation to a particular audience. The classical means of studying rhetoric remains a model for teaching people to use language, to think through ideas and to influence others in matters of politics and law. College public speaking courses use neo-Aristotelian concepts to teach students, interested in a broad range of professions, how to be effective speakers and listeners. Speech writers, working in political and public relations offices, are also likely to use neo-Aristotelian guidelines to determine if and how a given speech will be effective. Even though our teachers may not have identified their theoretical perspective, many of them have taught us how to deliver speeches and write essays according to this classical view.

The Western world savored Aristotle's very practical guide to the art of persuasion, although his *Rhetoric,* and works that are based on it, are equally useful as critical tools.[4] Neo-Aristotelian principles empower us by imploring us to consider all of the ways we are influenced by rhetoric, including *style, organization, rhetorical argument, ethos,* and *pathos.* This book devotes a chapter to each of these neo-Aristotelian concepts.

Critical Concepts Rooted in
Other Theories of Communication

The classical concepts presented here can be used with a variety of other concepts or independently. Communication continues to be vital to active democratic life, but communication technologies, philosophies, and education have changed. Rhetoric has become much more than public speech. The principles and goals of traditional rhetorical theories remain relevant in that they have been usefully applied to thinking critically about conversations, films, and written forms of communication. However, a good critical thinker should not ignore the wealth of theoretical concepts provided by other perspectives.

Some of the interpretive concepts suggested in these pages have been developed in Marxist theories that highlight the ways communication is ideological and oppressive. Concepts such as *narrative structure, narrative rationality,* and the *dramatistic pentad* are rooted in dramaturgical theories that frame all communication as storytelling or drama. Semiological concepts, also presented here, cast everything as potentially communicative.

As we make our way through the critical vocabulary, we will soon realize that one message can be interpreted in different ways. Some of the critical terminology will feel more comfortable or natural depending on whether one is critically reflecting on a speech, a television program, or a musical refrain. And some critics are more comfortable with some concepts than others. The final chapter of the book will present some of the ways critics choose among the interpretive vocabulary. For now, we are focused on the general process of interpretation, a process that should move the critic into evaluating the ways we make our lives meaningful.

Interpretation, the last sentence suggests, leads to an evaluation of communication. Critical evaluation depends on analysis and interpretation to explain and justify the evaluation. The process of thinking critically about communication is often described as beginning with an analysis of communication, moving through an interpretation of how people in the communication situation make sense of the communication, and concluding with judgment. The claim that one should reserve judgment until the final phase of criticism is ideal and it assumes judgments should—or could—be made as part of a linear, objective procedure. More significantly, thinking of judgment as the final phase of criticism is not particularly helpful because in many situations, judgment motivates critical thinking. In actuality, the three phases of criticism are interdependent. We should direct our thoughts to include some analysis, some interpretation, and some evaluation. A good critic must also be willing to revise his or her critical judgment if it cannot be sustained through rigorous critical thought.

▓▓▓▓ An Illustration of Critical Thinking

Because we have yet to discuss specific concepts for interpreting communication, this illustration is more of an outline of the overall process and
value of communication criticism. Several years ago, my students and I
attended all of the sessions of a local criminal rape trial. The defendant
was a 26-year-old man charged with, and acquitted for, raping a 20-year-
old woman. Our initial response to the jury's verdict was one of surprise
as we were convinced the man was guilty and that the prosecutor
presented an effective case. After thinking about the communication
critically, we came to understand a bit more about the law, our community, and ourselves.

When we first considered the arguments presented by the prosecutors
and defenders, we considered all statements made in the courtroom as
part of the communication text. We considered the communication
context, although in haste, to include the constraints of the courtroom
and legal procedures (part of a discursive formation), as well as the
professional notoriety of the prosecutor in this small city in upstate New
York. The jury was a mix of men and women, ranging in age from 25 to
60. Because this city includes many colleges and universities, half of the
jury consisted of college professors. We can safely assume that all of the
people on the jury are opposed to rape and violence, although they may
have different definitions of what constitutes rape. In this case, a definition of rape was not an issue. Some prejudices may exist toward college
students, who can be rowdy, but neither the plaintiff nor the defendant
was a student. Our interpretative and evaluative claim was that the
prosecutor made an effective and truthful case against the young man by
presenting an overwhelming amount of physical evidence that he was the
rapist: His fingerprints were on a Pepsi can in the woman's apartment,
his semen was on the sleeping bag in which the rape took place, and his
shirt was torn from his body by the victim as he was leaving the scene.

A more thoughtful critique of the communication at the trial steered
us to some different insights. Most significant was a closer study of the
jury's supertext. Specifically, the jury of locals had probably known about
a widely publicized case that took place a year earlier. In that case, local
police officers were found guilty of planting evidence in a murder case.
Although the "officers gone bad" were never mentioned at this trial, the
belief that many officers are guilty of evidence tampering most likely
interfered with the prosecution's case. The prosecutor put the police

officers who collected the evidence of the rape on the stand and questioned their procedures and motives. The defense attorney's cross-examination was quick. He simply asked where the evidence was kept after it was collected and who might have access to it. The jury learned that most of the evidence was not under lock and key at the precinct. My students and I realized that the jury had to believe all police at the precinct were trustworthy in order to accept any of the physical evidence. Only one juror needed to question the trustworthiness of only one officer, on or off this particular case, to raise the possibility of evidence tampering. Given the audience's supertext, it is likely that one or more jurors did doubt the integrity of the local police and a reasonable doubt freed the accused man.

My students and I learned several things from this exercise in critical thinking. We were able to understand why the prosecution was ineffective and how the jury came to acquit the accused. We learned that our community does not accept the authority of its police without question (all of this took place several years prior to the accusations against the police in the Rodney King and O. J. Simpson cases). We learned that we, at least initially, accepted the word of the police without question. We learned that we are easily convinced by what is called physical or factual evidence and that we should question the source of evidence.

Now, post-King and post-Simpson, I reconsider the local rape trial. I have come to see it as part of a historical struggle in which we are working through our beliefs and knowledge about, and actions regarding, race. The accused rapist was an African American man. The supertext of police evidence tampering, which probably influenced the jury, involved sending an African American woman to jail based on faulty fingerprints. I mention these details now because the intervening years and supertexts reshaped the context of this trial. Race seems more relevant now than it did then. Did my students and I question the word of the accused because he was African American and we are Caucasian? Did the jury consider the defendant's race as a factor that might have motivated the police to tamper with the evidence? Why didn't my students and I see race as being particularly relevant in the trial at the time? How much of our own racial identity influenced what we saw? And how much would I see race as being relevant even today if I had not been exposed to issues of race through other communication texts?

As meaning is itself always being rewritten, the critical process is never absolute or complete. One critic could never capture the entire workings of a film or speech. Consequently, there is a need for ongoing critical dialogue so that we may maintain control over the meanings in our lives. The next several chapters suggest a vocabulary to push the dialogue further.

Notes

1. For opposing views on defining texts worthy of critical attention, see Bloom (1987), and Gates (1992).

2. See Richard Vatz (1973/1995) on the argument that rhetoric creates situations more than it responds to them.

3. The following sources provide an introduction to the study of rhetoric in western civilization: Brummett (1994, Chap. 2); Gill (1994); Golden, Berquist, and Coleman (1992). Much of the interpretive vocabulary presented in these pages comes from this classical-rhetorical view of communication. The classical perspective provides a comprehensive and accessible theory for developing critical interpretive skills. Today we use the term "neo-Aristotelian" in reference to how history has engaged the ideas of many classical thinkers who studied communication, most notably, Plato, Aristotle, and Cicero. Aristotle's name has come to be associated with classical thinking because the ideas of others are traced to or from the theory of communication outlined in his *Rhetoric*.

4. Herbert Wichelns (1925/1995) wrote an essay on the difference between the criticism of spoken and written communication. The distinctions he drew were part of the academic split between departments of Speech Communication and English. The former developed and adapted Aristotelian concepts to guide the criticism of speech. The neo-Aristotelian approach to speech criticism that dominated departments of Speech Communication for 50 years is best summarized in Thonssen, Baird, and Braden (1970).

Reference List For Unit I

Agard, W. (1960). *What democracy meant to the Greeks.* Madison: University of Wisconsin Press.

Althusser, L. (1971). *Lenin and philosophy and other essays.* (B. Brewster, Trans.). London: New Left.

Aristotle. (1954). *Rhetoric.* (W. Rhys Roberts, Trans.). New York: Random House.

Belsey, C. (1980). *Critical practice.* New York: Methuen. Berkeley: University of California Press.

Bitzer, L. (1968). The rhetorical situation. *Philosophy and Rhetoric, 1,* 1-14.

Bloom, A. (1987). *The closing of the American mind.* New York: Simon & Schuster.

Brummett, B. (1994). *Rhetoric in popular culture.* New York: St. Martin's.

Buchanan, P. (1992). The election is about who we are (speech). *Vital Speeches of the Day, 52,* 712-717.

Campbell, K. K., & Jamieson, K. H. (1976). Form and genre in rhetorical criticism: An introduction. In K. K. Campbell, & K. H. Jamieson (Eds.), *Form and genre: Shaping rhetorical action* (pp. 9-32). Falls Church, VA: Speech Communication Association.

Cicero, M. T. (1970). *De oratore.* (J.S. Watson, Trans.). Carbondale: Southern Illinois University Press.

Eagleton, T. (1976). *Marxism and literary criticism.* Berkeley: University of California Press.

Fiske, J. (1987). British cultural studies and television. In R. C. Allen (Ed.), *Channels of discourse* (pp. 254-289). Chapel Hill: University of North Carolina Press.

Fiske, J. (1989). *Reading the popular.* Boston: Unwin Hyman.

Foucault, M. (1972). *The archeology of knowledge.* (A. M. Sheridan Smith, Trans.). New York: Harper & Row.

Friedan, B. (1981). *The second stage.* New York: Summit.

Garlake, P. (1982). *Great Zimbabwe described and explained.* Harare, Zimbabwe: Zimbabwe Publishing House.

Gates, H. L. (1992). *Loose canons: Notes on the culture wars.* New York: Oxford University Press.

Geertz, C. (1973). *Interpretation of cultures.* New York: Basic Books.

Gill, A. (1994). *Rhetoric and human understanding.* Prospect Heights, IL: Waveland Press.

Golden, J. L., Berquist, G. F., & Coleman, W. E. (1992). *The rhetoric of western thought* (5th ed.). Dubuque, IA: Kendall/Hunt.

Grmek, M. D. (1990). *History of AIDS.* (R. C. Maulitz & J. Duffin, Trans.). Princeton, NJ: Princeton University Press.

Grossberg, L. (1987). The in-difference of television. *Screen, 28,* 33.

Hall, S. (1985). Signification, representation, ideology, Althusser and the post-structuralist debates. *Critical Studies in Mass Communication, 2,* 91-114.

Johnston, J. (1973). *Lesbian nation: The feminist solution.* New York: Simon & Schuster.

Marx K. (1961). *Marx on economics.* (R. Freedman, Ed.). New York: Harcourt Brace.

Marx, K., & Engels, F. (1973). *Marx and Engels on literature and art.* (L. Bacandall & S. Morawski, Eds.). St. Louis, MO: Telos Press.

Maugham, S. (1944). *The razor's edge.* Toronto: W. Heinemann.

Morley, D. (1989). Changing paradigms in audience studies. In E. Sieter, H. Beorchers, G. Kruetzner, & E. Warth (Eds.), *Remote control: Television, audiences, and cultural power* pp. 16-41. New York: Routledge.

Plato (1981). *Five dialogues.* (G. M. A. Grube, Trans.). Indianapolis, IN: Hackett Publishing.

Raspberry, W. (1991). The role of racism in black poverty is exaggerated. In W. Dudley (Ed.), *Racism in America* (pp. 85-92). San Diego, CA: Greenhaven Press.

Thonssen, L., Baird, A. G., & Braden, W. W. (1970). *Speech criticism* (2nd ed.). New York: Ronald Press.

Vatz, R. E. (1995). The myth of the rhetorical situation. In W. Covino & D. Jolliffee (Eds.), *Rhetoric: concepts, definitions, boundaries* (pp. 461-467). Boston: Allyn & Bacon. (Reprinted from *Philosophy and rhetoric, 6,* 1973)

Waller, R. J. (1995). *The bridges of Madison County.* New York: Warner Books.

White, M. (1987). Ideological analysis and television. In R. C. Allen (Ed.), *Channels of discourse* (pp. 134-171). Chapel Hill: University of North Carolina Press.

Wichelns, H. A. (1995). The literary criticism of oratory. In C. Burgchardt (Ed.), *Readings in rhetorical criticism* (pp. 3-28). State College, PA: Strata Publishing. (Reprinted from A. M. Drummond (Ed.). *Studies in rhetoric and public speaking in honor of James Albert Winans.* New York: Century, 1925)

Williams, Patricia (1991). *The alchemy of race and rights.* Cambridge, MA: Harvard University Press. Indianapolis, IN: Hackett Publishing.

UNIT ▌▌

CRITICAL CONCEPTS THAT
FOCUS ON LANGUAGE

The concepts presented here, and in the following three units, suggest different ways to critically frame communication. The critical concepts are arranged around five components of communication that shape meaning: language, structure, reasoning, character and emotion. Critical concepts can be thought of as filters that bring some features of meaningful communication to the fore, while relegating other dimensions of meaning to the background. Although the units and chapters could be read in a different order, we begin with language because it is the most basic component of all human communication and therefore communication criticism.

In this book, the term language is used broadly to include all forms of expression that come to have shared meanings for groups of people. Language obviously includes verbal forms of speech and writing, but colors, film-frames, images, objects, physical gestures, facial expressions, sounds, smells, textures, and size become full of meaning. Many different kinds of language work together when people engage in a conversation, create a film, or present speeches.

We are also concerned with the many shades or dimensions of meaning. For instance, $ means money. The word *money* refers to currency that is exchanged for goods and services. The word money also has meaningful associations, such as value and wealth. Typically, symbolic representations of money occur in contexts that influence the meaning of the dollar sign, word, or actual object. In our culture, money is greatly valued; we believe it should be earned through hard work; and that one can express love for another person by spending a lot of money on that person. People create these meanings through recurring contexts from parents giving a child an allowance to advertisements that say, "If it is true love, you will buy her the best diamond."

A good critic is attentive to all language and the many possible ways it comes to have meaning for people. This unit casts language into three different frameworks that are useful for thinking critically about language. They are critical tools that may be used alone or in combination with one another, concepts presented in the other units, or both. The first framework, "language as style," was established by classical thinkers and adapted by contemporary teachers as a guide to teach effective speaking and writing. Rather than present **style** as a how-to guide to speaking and writing well, Chapter 3 considers stylistic qualities as a guide to thinking critically about language, particularly words. The second framework, known as **semiotics,** (Chap. 4) extends language to include almost anything. For example, semiotics allows you to critically consider how a table setting shapes meaning. The final framework, **metaphor,** (Chap. 5) is not distinct from theories of style or semiotics. Metaphors require special attention because many great thinkers share in the belief that all meaning is metaphorical.

3 Language as Style

Style is one of several critical approaches to language that will be discussed in this unit. Style is the verbal clothing of ideas. The ancient study of rhetoric developed theories of style or *elocutio* to explain how to use spoken words to inform and influence people. A good speaker was advised to use words appropriately, accurately, vividly, and clearly. Our educational system continues to teach students how to speak and write according to the traditional principles of style.

In more recent times (1920s-1960s), communication teachers adopted and adapted Aristotelian theories of style for the critical study of speeches. These neo-Aristotelian critics emphasized the referential and symbolic nature of words (Stewart, 1972). The referential nature of symbols locates meaning in the ideas, things, or behaviors to which words refer. This view calls attention to the difference between words, ideas, and things. The symbolic nature of words is in their conventional and arbitrary relationship to their referents. In English, the word *dog*, for instance, came to mean the four-legged domesticated animal through custom rather than some necessary, or natural, relationship between the word and the thing. It is the arbitrariness of symbolic meanings that make them particularly interesting to the critical thinker who asks what, how, and why some meanings prevail. Symbolic meanings involve the imagination and cooperation of audiences who agree to make sense of them. The critical study of style, therefore, is a study of people and their ideas.

The Aristotelian roots of style give it a practical, or functional, angle. The practical schools of speech ask how words influence an audience's beliefs and actions. They are interested in the realities that are made in talk. For some people, the realities produced in talk are "social" realities, consisting of conceptual beliefs, attitudes, and values that are different from facts or "objective" realities. For others, such as Foss (1989), language produces the only reality we know because "we have or know a reality only through the language by which we describe it. We constitute reality through our symbols" (p. 188). Kenneth Burke's (1966) idea that language is a "terministic screen" (Chap. 3) is yet another way to understand how language shapes the world we live in. Accordingly, we come to know the world through language, which is a screen that directs and deflects attention.

Michael Leff's (1988/1995) study of President Lincoln's *Second Inaugural Address* illustrates how style directed perceptions of the Civil War and shaped postwar policy. In the speech, Lincoln had to make sense of the war in a way that would allow the country to reunite and rebuild. His use of language frames the war as an act of divine intervention. Specifically, his choice of verb tense, arrangement of sentences, paragraphs, tone, and imagery construct the public and the president as passive and forgiving beings. Lincoln begins his speech with sentences that move from past tense, to present tense, to the future tense. He then builds paragraphs into this same pattern. Lincoln uses few personal pronouns in this address, and the passive voice "creates the impression that the occasion . . . renders him captive and passive" (p. 527). As he moves from past events to the present and future, he uses an increasing amount of religious imagery by quoting the Bible and referring to prayer. In so doing, he brings the secular events of the past war into a vision of sacred time, which is timeless and beyond history. This combination of stylistic factors renders the audience passive with respect to blaming others for the past. It renders the audience presently dutiful to God. And it pushes the audience to mold the future in the frame of Christian virtues.

Critics of style, such as Leff, frame language and meaning in ways that include a variety of critical interests, goals, and assumptions. The study of style is no longer limited to speeches or even to words. Symbol systems other than words, such as film images or musical rhythms, are not formal languages, but we may nevertheless interpret them from a stylistic perspective. After all, the film directors Alfred Hitchcock, Frank Capra, Steven Spielberg, and Quentin Tarantino have their own styles. We are familiar with conversational styles, musical styles, and teaching styles. Here, I emphasize the neo-Aristotelian view of style because it offers a perspective that is not evident in other ways of viewing language.[1] Critical thinkers, who use the concept style, share a vocabulary for describing how language directs and deflects attention. This functional approach to style can be clarified by first understanding what style *is*.

The Qualities of Style

Throughout the history of Western civilization, scholars from Ancient Greece to contemporary America have identified the qualities of effective style.[2] Different sources present different qualities, but most discussions are variations of the theme that language should be **correct, clear, appropriate, and vivid** (Thonssen, Baird, & Braden, 1970, Chap. 16). The differences among theories of style are primarily found in the name and number of stylistic qualities identified. Aristotle, the ancient Greek philosopher, dedicates Book III of the *Rhetoric* to style, including a discussion of clear style, appropriate style, rhythmic style, impressive style, and lively style. Cicero, a Roman statesman, orator, and scholar, highlights correctness, clarity, ornateness, and propriety (*De Oratore*, Book III). After retiring from teaching in 1783, Hugh Blair, an 18th-century professor of rhetoric, published his *Lectures on Rhetoric and Belles Lettres*. Twenty of the 47 lectures are specifically about style. In them, he draws heavily on the works of Aristotle, Cicero, and other classical theorists, emphasizing simplicity and a lively imagination. Aristotle and Blair's discussions of "liveliness" are similar to Cicero's "ornateness." Aristotle approaches "correctness" as part of "clarity" more than as an independent quality.

The differences among the qualities scholars identify as effective style are, for the most part, insignificant. A critic will prefer one system of laying out the qualities of effective style to the others. Some variation of the four qualities of effective style, to be discussed here, can be found in any contemporary public-speaking textbook and most introductory writing textbooks.[3]

The Qualities of Correctness and Clarity

Correctness of speech refers to whether the speaker uses words accurately, including proper grammatical structure. A more complex undertaking of the quality of correctness, and one which draws on the referential nature of meaning, considers whether the speaker's words are faithful to the speaker's thoughts and to the world of facts.

A clear style is one that conveys the speaker's intended meaning to the audience. **Clarity** necessitates using words that are familiar to the audience and typically words that are specific and unambiguous. Americans tend to value directness of style in most communication situations. In a direct style, the speaker identifies herself and her audience, rather than speaking passively. In a direct style, the speaker also makes her purpose and points obvious to the audience. A clear style is often aided by "methods of amplification," that is, word choices and word arrangements that emphasize and enliven ideas. Some commonly used methods of amplification include the following:

a. *Parallel structure* repeats the grammatical structure of a sentence two or more times. For instance, Elizabeth Taylor, the actress, used parallel structure in a speech she gave, as Chair of the American Foundation for AIDS Research, to a congressional task force (1990):

The CARE bill will provide emergency relief to our cities hardest hit by AIDS. The bill will also provide comprehensive care for all people with AIDS and HIV infection throughout the country.

The CARE bill will also allow people to receive treatment and care in their homes. That is so much more humane and less expensive than hospital care. More importantly, the CARE bill will help pay for crucial early treatment for AIDS and HIV disease. (p. 72)

b. *Antithesis* contrasts ideas within a sentence, or consecutive sentences. Jesse Jackson (1984) used the following antithesis in his *Rainbow Coalition* speech: "The team that got us here must be expanded, not abandoned" (p. 358).

c. *Anaphora* repeats a key word or words throughout the communication text or a part of it. In his 1992 *Address to the Republican Convention,* Pat Buchanan used variations on the phrase 'coming home,' as in "This party is my home. This party is our home, and we've got to come home to it."

d. *Alliteration* repeats the same sound two or more times within a sentence or consecutive sentences. Alliterations come in two types, *assonance,* which repeats vowel sounds, and *consonance,* which repeats consonants. Martin Luther King, always stylistically poetic, used alliteration almost all of the time. The following sentence from his *I Have a Dream* speech (1963) repeats the "s" sound: "I have a dream that one day even the state of Mississippi, a desert state sweltering with the heat of injustice and oppression, will be transformed into an oasis of freedom and justice" (p. 80).

The Qualities of Appropriateness and Vividness

The third quality of good style, **appropriateness,** requires the speaker to adapt his style to the communication context. Words carry a tone or mood that should fit the situation. The medium of communication will, for instance, suggest an appropriate tone. The style of a telephone conversation with one colleague will be more informal than the style of a public presentation given to colleagues at a conference.

Finally, a **vivid** style creates images in the minds of the audience. Figures of speech use words in imaginative and nonliteral ways to embellish ideas. The following are some commonly used figures of speech:

a. *Metaphors and similes* connect or equate ideas that are dissimilar. *Similes* are explicit comparisons, such as "Our laundry detergent is like a breath of fresh air." *Metaphors* explicitly or implicitly say that two things are the same. The simile becomes an explicit metaphor in "Our laundry detergent is a breath of fresh air." In an implicit metaphor, the advertiser suggests the detergent is fresh air by having the personified box of detergent blow wind on a pile of dirty clothes. Songs and other poetic forms of communication often include metaphors and similes. The song *Strange Fruit,* written by Lewis Allen (1939) and made popular by the great Blues singer Billie Holiday, compares the bodies of Blacks who have been lynched to rotting fruit.

b. *Metonymy* is a type of metaphor that substitutes a word associated with an idea or thing for the idea or thing itself. For instance, Faye Wattleton (1991), president of Planned Parenthood from 1978-1991, refers to gender relationships in 1950s America as the "Father Knows Best syndrome" (p. 131), using a popular television program of that time to reflect life at that time.

c. *Synecdoche,* a related concept, uses part of a concept for the whole as in "sail" for "boat," and "president" for "the government."

Figures of speech are not the only path to vividness. A clear and precise vocabulary, an active grammatical structure, and evidence in the form of examples are some other ways to achieve vividness.

The Functions of Style

This traditional view, focusing on the qualities of effective style, can be formal and static. I. A. Richards (1965), a contemporary philosopher who wrote about language and meaning, says the qualities of effective style are not helpful to anyone interested in promoting human understanding because they simply classify. He, in fact, suggests the qualities of style, as traditionally studied are "trivialities":

> Instead of a philosophic inquiry into how words work in discourse, we get the usual postcard's-worth of crude common sense:—Be clear, yet don't be dry; be vivacious, use metaphors when they will be understood not otherwise; respect usage; don't be long-winded, on the other hand don't be gaspy; avoid ambiguity; prefer the energetic to the elegant; preserve unity and coherence. (p. 8)

Richards directs attention from what style is to how words work. This shift in attention does not mean we have to abandon the qualities of style. Rather than take an inventory of style, a critic can explore how communicators achieve the qualities and with what effects. This "functional approach" to style is interested in how a speaker creates images, clarity, or rhythm with words, and how these stylistic qualities may influence and/or reflect the ideas and identities of the speaker, the audience, or both. Once the critic interprets how style functioned in the situation, he or she will be prepared to make some critical evaluations.

Critical Questions and Answers

The best way to summarize how style can be a critical tool is to present some generally phrased questions a critic using this concept would ask and to illustrate how a few communication critics have answered the questions. The critical questions should be thought of as a "heuristic" device. A heuristic is something that stimulates thinking and discovery. The critical questions should help you think critically about the functions of style. There are no absolute answers to any of these questions and the critic may answer one or all of them. Notice how the illustrative answers include an understanding of the audience and make use of the interpretive vocabulary of style.

1. **Does the speaker's use of style effectively achieve his or her purpose? Explain.**

    Critical comment on effectiveness: In 1976, *Playboy* magazine published an interview with President Jimmy Carter in which the president makes several statements about sex and marriage. Much of the public responded to the interview with reproach. In a critical study of the interview, Martha Solomon (1978) explains the negative response to be a result of Carter's inappropriate style. Solomon illustrates how, in the interview, Carter shifted from a cordial and restrained style to an informal and intimate style. She concludes, "The crux of Carter's problem in the final phase of the interview was that he moved from a stylistic level which met the expectations of voters for his role and image to a more personal and informal level of style which disappointed their expectations. . . . Although he did have the personal relationship with Scheer (the interviewer) to make the change acceptable in the immediate context, he did not have the close contact with the public as a whole to make such a personal tone appropriate" (p. 180).

2. **Does the speaker use style that presents himself, the world, or both, truthfully and ethically? Explain.**

    Critical comment on truth and ethics: President Nixon presented a plan for removing American troops from Vietnam, in his *Vietnamization* speech (1969).[4] In her critical study of the speech, Karlyn Kohrs Campbell (1972) argues that Nixon compromises his ethics as his words intentionally misrepresent his public opposition and the history of Vietnam. He "misrepresents his opposition by treating them as a homogeneous group who seek immediate, precipitate withdrawal." In reality, Campbell says, Nixon's critics favored a variety of methods for ending the war and most of them opposed immediate withdrawal. "A second misrepresentation occurs in relation to what the president calls the 'fundamental issue. Why and how did the United States become involved in Vietnam in the first place?' " Nixon's description of the beginning of the war is disputable. The president claims that in 1954, North Vietnam was being backed by Communist China and the Soviet Union. But in actuality, the North Vietnamese did not gain the communist backing until 1959, whereas the United States was involved in Vietnamese politics in 1954 (Campbell, p. 51).

Critical comment on truth and ethics: In a more recent critical study of style in Spike Lee's *Do the Right Thing,* Detine L. Bowers (1994) illustrates that Lee's characters' stylistic use of time, structure, improvisation, and call-response accurately reflect an Afrocentric use of language, and an Afrocentric worldview.

3. **How does the speaker's use of style shape identities, ideas, and/or actions?**

Critical comment on identities, ideas, and actions: Campbell (1972) claims the most significant problem with Nixon's *Vietnamization* speech is that it perpetuates false myths about the identity of America, which could lead to actions that will ultimately "destroy us" (p. 57). The president describes a mythical America that "seeks justice, freedom and right despite difficulty and cost." But nonmythical America "supports totalitarian governments," is engaging in a war that "is systematically destroying the civilian population," and "practices racism" (p. 56).

Critical comment on identities, ideas, and actions: Jack Lule (1995) studies the images evoked from newspaper descriptions of heavyweight boxer Mike Tyson's rape trial. He argues that the words unanimously and uniformly portray two identities for Tyson: "He was either a crude, sex-obsessed, violent savage who could barely control his animal instinct or he was a victim of terrible social circumstances. . . . Both portraits depict a man without self-control or determination, paradoxical for a former world champion" (p. 181).

I deliberately selected critical studies that do not attend to all of the questions listed. For instance, Campbell is not interested in whether Nixon's speech was effective. Solomon is interested in the effectiveness of Carter's style but questions of truth or ethics are not particularly relevant. And yet all of the examples give us some insight into the ways communication shapes our realities. Solomon's critical thinking about the interview with Carter shows us how culture uses language to establish and maintain a social situation. Her study also suggests that individual speaking style, a series of choices made by the speaker, presents an identity to others that can be accepted or rejected, because it is or is not consistent with how others view (or want to view) the speaker.

Although Campbell and Bowers make judgments about truth, they also make assertions about the ideas and identities of those who participate in communication. Campbell blames Nixon for attempting to create an American identity that, according to her, does not exist and should not exist. She is, in effect, asking Americans, "Is this who we want to be, and if so, what kind of actions will it lead to?" Bowers's critique acknowledges and celebrates African American identity in two key ways. First, Bowers adapts the qualities and functions of style to appreciate Spike Lee's representation of African American forms of speech. Second, Bowers illustrates how African American audiences have a distinct set of experiences and ideas through which they will make sense of the film's language.·

In short, to think about style critically is to consider how people use words in a particular context, whether they are used effectively, truthfully, ethically, and whether or not they generate desirable effects. Style is a concept most easily applied to thinking about written and spoken words. We have seen, however, that style can be adapted to the critical study of film and be sensitive to different cultural styles. The critical thinker, however, cannot know the best means of critically examining language without considering several options.

Notes

1. More specifically, the neo-Aristotelian perspective on style (more than semiology or metaphor) allows the critic to make representational assumptions about the relationship between language and ideas, and language and things. It also invites the critic to assume that language expresses the persona of the speaker. Style can also be a useful concept for critics who believe language is constitutive of meaning. The final chapter discusses these assumptions and their relationship to critical thinking.

2. In addition to the primary sources noted here, see Golden, Berquist, and Coleman, 1992, for an historical overview of classical theories of style.

3. Arnold (1974), Blankenship (1968), and Thonssen, Baird, and Braden (1970) shaped the neoclassical approach to style of rhetorical criticism. Their works may serve as guides to critiquing style.

4. Nixon's *Vietnamization* speech generated much controversy among neo-Aristotelian critics. Karlyn Kohrs Campbell and Forbes Hill (1972) were two key figures in an academic debate over how to use Aristotle's *Rhetoric* to evaluate contemporary speeches. Much of the debate focused on the necessity to judge, or even the possibility of judging, the truth and ethics of a speaker's message.

4 Language as Sign Systems

Semiotics, the science of signs, casts language broadly.[1] Language is anything that signifies a concept. The something that signifies, officially termed the **signifier,** can be anything that people make meaningful, including words, objects, colors, smells, shapes, textures, and tastes. Semiotics invites the critical thinker to ignore the boundaries of intentional, symbolic-verbal communication and study all meaning. Film images, actors, dialogue, sound, lighting, and editing are signifiers available for semiotic interpretation. Semiotics invites us to critically unravel the signifiers of a holiday ritual such as Thanksgiving or the design of a clothing store.

Semiotics casts language in a different frame than does style. Semiotics brackets issues about truth or reality beyond meaningful communication that many referential approaches to language raise. In the previous chapter, for instance, we reviewed a critical study that claimed Nixon's words did not accurately represent people or historical events. A semiotic approach displaces the question of how words correspond to the world, by focusing on meaning as a mental process (Gottdiener, 1995, p.11). The semiotic framework imagines meaning as a process in which signifiers join signifieds in sign systems.

Signifiers become meaningful signs when people associate them with a concept, which is called a **signified.** Roland Barthes (1980), a French intellectual who studied meaning as sign systems, describes how the obese, sagging flesh of a wrestler's body is a signifier for his vileness

(1980, p.17). Kate Kane, a professor of communication, explains how cleanliness and freshness have become signifiers of a feminine identity in American culture (1990). Gaye Tuchman and Harry Levine (1993), sociologists interested in the semiotics of culture, explain that for Jewish Americans "eating in Chinese restaurants signifies that one is not a provincial or parochial Eastern European Jew, not a 'greenhorn' or hick" (p.385). Semiotics can reveal the ways eating rituals build cultural identity and ideology.

One sign relationship, such as cleanliness signifying femininity or eating Chinese food signifying sophistication, is only a microscopic part of the meaning process. Signs combine themselves with other signs into systems of meaning, or ideologies. Thinking critically with semiotics is similar to opening an accordion and examining each fold and its connection to every other fold of the instrument. For instance, a semiotic study of a standard photograph in a high school yearbook would attempt to account for how the subject's hair style, hair color, clothing style, texture, colors, facial features, make-up, expressions, background lighting, and the frame of the photo work together to create its meaning(s). A full-blown semiotic study of just one communication text could take years. That does not mean semiotics is useless to everyday critical thinkers. Semiotics allows us to see the communication that is everywhere: in the ways we prepare food, construct buildings, and make a walk in the woods a meaningful experience. Even the most cursory understanding of semiotics can kindle critical thinking.

The following sections provide a fundamental vocabulary for thinking about how signs shape meaning. Whereas a critical view of style focuses on the qualities and functions of language, the semiotic approach is best described as meaningful relationships or associations. As in the previous chapter, we will conclude by illustrating some critical questions and answers, and some of the advantages and disadvantages of working semiotically.

Semiotic Relationships

Signs transform themselves through several relationships, and meaning flourishes. A critic examines the relationships within, between, and among **signifiers, signifieds,** and **signs.** For the professional semiologist, the interpretation of sign relationships is a technical and tedious process.

In this section, I group the numerous and often minute relationships that the critic should attend to into three general relational categories: signifier to signified, signifier from other signifiers, and signs with signs.

Associations Between Signifiers and Signifieds

The first set of relationships, often referred to as the denotative level of meaning, is found in the ways people connect signifiers to signifieds. Signifiers that have an arbitrary relationship with their signifieds are **symbolically** connected. As was mentioned previously, most words are arbitrarily associated with their concepts. Flags arbitrarily signify countries. The television picture fading to black between camera shots arbitrarily represents a shift in scene. Signifiers that have a similarity to their signifieds are **iconically** connected. Onomatopoeic words, such as **thud,** bear similarity to our experiences. Photographic images are iconically related to the subject of the photo. The pillars that seem to support the administration building on a college campus are icons of the columns in Ancient Greek architecture. Signifiers that have a natural or material link to their signifieds are **indexically** connected. The smell of smoke is an index for burning. The trail of blood that followed you from the crime scene indexically signifies your involvement in the crime. Taking an entire day to prepare a meal indexically signifies that the meal is special.

Understanding the variety of connections between signifiers and signifieds helps us realize the richness of meaning. Any signifier may be simultaneously symbolic, iconic, and indexical. For instance, a television campaign advertisement for Ronald Reagan's presidency in 1984 featured an image of a grizzly bear roaming in the woods. The image of the bear is an icon of the animal bear, an index of danger and a symbol of the Soviet Union. Of course, audiences do not necessarily make all of the connections consciously or perhaps even unconsciously. The critical thinker can only unravel semiotic relationships through the people who make sense of them. An audience of 50-year-olds may share the symbolic meaning of the bear, whereas an audience of 20-year-olds may not.

Comparisons of the Signifiers to Potential Signifiers

As quickly as signifier and signified become a sign, people transform them into signifiers for a cultural value or connotation. For instance, a photograph of a child can be viewed as a signifier. The first order of signification is an iconic representation of a "real" child. The second order of signification associates the concept of the child with its cultural values. In American culture, a child signifies innocence. The second order of meaning can be found in the differences between a given signifier and potential signifiers of the same ilk. In the case of the photographed child, the critical thinker arrives at the connotative sign "innocence" by considering the signifiers that are not present. The child in the photograph is not several children, a teenager, an adult, or an elderly person. The child differs from these potential signifiers, within the same category, in its innocence. If the child is wearing a red dress, the critic should ask how the signifier *red* is different from other signifiers in the paradigm of colors; and how a dress may have cultural associations that are different from overalls or pajamas. The critic who explores the road not taken is on his or her way to unraveling ideologies.

Connections Among Signs

The cultural belief, or explanation, for the transformation from child to innocence is the third order of signification. The child in the photograph becomes innocence because "children are good, simple, and by nature moral." The third sign is an idea—or a cultural myth—that, when combined with other signs, forms an ideology. When critically exploring this level of meaning, you attend to how signs are positioned with other signs. Imagine that the child in the photograph is placed in front of an American flag. Or perhaps the background of the photograph is colored in red, white, and blue. In either case, childhood and innocence become associated with America. Cultural myths about childhood—children are good, simple, and by nature moral—become associated with myths about America—in America, people are free. When signs repeatedly show up together, as images of children and America often do, they suggest an ideology or a system of unquestioned cultural equations among America, innocence, youth, morality, and freedom.

Signs of women in advertising provide many examples of how recurring sign combinations shape ideas and identities. Signs of women often appear with signs of sexuality, such as erotic poses, and signs of desirable objects, such as automobiles. The semiotic argument is that such a combination of signs, although not necessarily intentionally designed, interpellates the communicators into an ideology that equates sexual desire and the desire to own things (consumership): The desire to own things is natural; owning an automobile satisfies desire; automobiles are status symbols; women are objects to be possessed; women are status symbols; owning women brings pleasure.

The method of semiotic interpretation is quite detailed, but we should not allow ourselves to get too bogged down in technique because sometimes denotative meanings dominate and other times audiences will skip over denotative meanings in favor of second and third orders of meaning. Further, there is so much meaning in human experience that no one critic can capture it all. The questions that follow should be a heuristic for using semiology as a critical process that allows us more choice in our identities, beliefs, and behaviors. After some practice, we will find ourselves interpreting the meaning that is everywhere.

█████ Critical Questions and Answers

Before tackling the critical questions, we must put some boundaries around the text and context we are interpreting. The boundaries are not too much of a problem if the text is a public speech. However, if we are interested in how people shape the meanings in wrestling matches or cultural rituals, we must decide what to include as part of the so-called communication text and surrounding context. A semiotic study of Halloween could examine the sign systems active at a specific Halloween party but it could also consider the more generic sign systems that make Halloween a cultural holiday. We could think about the food, costumes, acts, and colors as signifiers, or narrow our critical thinking to costumes or a particular costume that is popular among children.

The next phase of a semiological reading of any communication is to move through the sign systems methodically. As a review of the process, consider how Roland Barthes (1980) uses semiology to examine how the images in a French cooking magazine, *Elle,* appeal to its working-class readers. He first looks at signifiers in the photograph that belong to the category of coatings, including sauces, creams and jellies. As first-order signifiers, the photographs of coated food in *Elle* iconically signify coatings of food. Barthes is more concerned with the second order of meaning in which an audience associates coatings with ornamentation, beauty, art, magic, and fantasy. To uncover the meaningful potential of the signifiers, Barthes differentiates between the category of "coated" foods featured in *Elle* magazine and the possibility of using "uncoated" foods as signifiers. He reasons that coated foods transform nature and reality into culture and fantasy: "A cookery which is based on coatings and alibis . . . is forever trying to extenuate and even to disguise the primary nature of foodstuffs, the brutality of meat or the abruptness of sea-food" (p. 78).

The signs become sign systems when the readers of the magazine no longer separate beliefs about food, consumption, and art. Sign systems are, in this sense, mythic or ideological. For instance, Barthes claims the ideology of *Elle* joins contradictory assumptions about food and ornamentation: Food is real; ornamentation is fantasy; food satisfies hunger; fantasies may often be satisfied through art; food is fantasy; ornamentation satisfies hunger.

Some of the critical conclusions Barthes makes in his study of *Elle* are reported in the critical comments that follow. Because the semiotic framework lays out how people think, it is most suitable to make judgments about the communicators' identities, ideas and actions; however, the vocabulary of semiotics may be adapted to questions of effectiveness and truth.

1. **Do the sign systems effectively fulfill the creator's (speaker, artist, culture's) purpose? Explain.**

Critical comment on effectiveness: Barthes (1980) acknowledges that *Elle's* images of food sell a fantasy, not food. "Its role is to present its vast public which (market-research tells us) is working class, the very dream of smartness" (p. 78). The appeal of smartness or class sells the magazine.

Critical comment on effectiveness: Ellen Seiter (1990) examines many different categories of signifiers in her study of how visual advertising constructs images of children. Though her essay focuses on the racism of the ads, she first acknowledges children are an effective way to sell products: "Babies are attention grabbers, they are especially good at catching the eyes of women consumers who so often constitute the target market. Perhaps most important for the cautious advertiser, children rarely offend" (p. 31).

2. **Do the sign systems present the world, or ideas about the world, truthfully and ethically? Explain.**

Critical comment on truth and ethics: Barthes claims *Elle's* food fantasy covers a material need with a cultural ideology. In Barthes's words, "The real problem is not to have the idea of sticking cherries into a partridge, it is to have the partridge, that is to say, to pay for it," and "The readers of *Elle* are entitled only to fiction" (p. 80).

Critical comment on truth and ethics: Seiter (1990) argues that general market advertisers typically join white babies and children with other signifiers for innocence, such as whiteness, soft lighting, and newness. Innocence and childhood are joined with a myth of safety signified by images of home and family. White children have access to the American Dream. Children of color are excluded from participating in the meaning of the American Dream through their exclusion from the ads. Seiter concludes, "Many advertisers treat minority consumers no better than Columbus treated the Indians centuries ago. The comparison is apt because media audiences today are indeed, like the Indians, an economic colony, exploited and disregarded by a dominant group with little interest in their culture" (p. 44).

Critical comment on truth and ethics: Seiter points out some deceptions in the ways media use white children, and children of color. Among them: "Television so often portrays suffering children as Black and Hispanic that it has been hard for the white middle class in the 1980s to comprehend the fact that staggering numbers of mothers and children who live in poverty are white" (p. 32).

3. **How do the sign systems shape identities, ideas, and actions?**

Critical comment on identities, ideas, and action: In *Elle*, the combination of food signs and coating signs relates beliefs about eating, consumption, and art. The working-class readers, according to Barthes, transform natural hunger into unreal fantasy; and the pleasure of visual images is substituted for the real satisfaction of food. *Elle* creates a desire and satisfies a fantasy for people who can buy the magazine but not much food. The transformation of meaning here may quell conflict between social classes more than it will quell hunger.

Critical comment on identities, ideas, and action: Seiter notes, "Children so often grow up to fulfill the status quo that the representation of children is especially good at 'naturalizing' social relations, by making unequal destinies seem inevitable." Referring to the images common in ads, she says, "After all, boys so often grow up to be boys. For the blonde blue-eyed laughing boy, advertisements project dreams of power and success. For the dancing, light-skinned Black girl no such future is ever envisioned" (p. 32).

The semiotic approach to language may be summarized as a micro-scopic look at the movement of meaning. Seemingly, all at once a signifier meets a signified in an indexical, symbolic, and/or iconic sign, the sign meets a cultural value, and the value is further transformed into a cultural belief that accounts for the relationship between first- and second-order sign. In this movement of meaning, called signification, meaning unfolds and plays back on itself like an accordion. The sign interacts with other signs, forming systems of meaning.

The overwhelming nature of thinking about language as a sign system is both a strength and a weakness. The critic can consider the communi-cative potential of anything that signifies something else. Language does not require purpose or intention to be meaningful. Though the technique of semiotics can be tedious, it can be quite revealing. Each of the critical studies described in this section uses semiology to move through who the signifiers appeal to and why, the audience's belief systems that are necessary to making sense of the signifiers, and the kinds of actions (or inactions) such beliefs can lead to.

Focusing on meaning as a mental process can be a problem because it does not explicitly connect communication to the world of affairs. For some people, the exclusion of "the real" makes semiotics an intellectual exercise with little value. Others are working on ways to integrate the material world (typically in the socioeconomic sense) into semiotics. Though I do not want to belabor the history of semiotics, I will draw on a couple of key theorists and issues in order to explain this philosophical puzzle.

Ferdinand de Saussure and Charles Sanders Peirce, to whom we trace the development of semiotics, offer different philosophical explanations for how signifiers join with signifieds into meaningful sign relationships. Saussure was a linguist, essentially interested in how people intentionally use verbal language to communicate. Similar to those who developed theories of effective style, he regarded the sounds and images of words as having an arbitrary and cultural relationship to their referents. In other words, there is no natural or essential reason why the word *dog* comes to mean the domesticated canine or "a cake with creamy icing" comes to mean beauty and wealth. Saussure's theory of language is most signifi-cantly different from other theories in his claim that it does not name things that already exist. Saussure believed language creates the distinc-tions that we come to see as objects in the world. The word *dog* allows us to notice dogs as something different from cats, rabbits, birds, and so on. In her explanation of Saussure on this point, Catherine Belsey (1980) writes,

> It is not that I cannot distinguish between shades of blue but that the language insists on a difference . . . between blue and green. The world, which without signification would be experienced as a continuum, is divided up by language into entities which then readily come to be experienced as essentially distinct. (p. 40)

In short, Saussure's theory of signs excludes reference to objective reality. Language is a sound or image and a socially agreed on thought about that sound/image.

Peirce, who wrote a theory of semiotics at the same time as Saussure (early 20th century) but independently of him, was a philosopher concerned with how science can give us knowledge about the objective world. Though his purpose was to understand language as a means of discovering and expressing truths, his theory of semiotics never fully accounts for how the "real" or "true" world participates in meaningful signs (Gottdiener, p. 10). Peirce's assumption of an objective world is, however, implied in his elaboration of Saussure's moment of signification. For Peirce, the person who joins signifier and signified must do so by relating the signifier to some previous experience in the world. Accordingly, the image of "icing on a cake" can only evoke the concept of the beauty and fantasy if the interpreter has had some experience with cakes and icing. The objective world also enters into Peirce's theory of signs in his assertion that the relationship between signifier and signified is not limited to arbitrary representations. People may join signifiers to signifieds because they bear a natural resemblance or association to their experiences in the material word. For instance, a cartoon image looks just like the president and a sore throat comes to be associated with an illness. Of course, the objective, natural, real, or material world enters Peirce's scheme in the form of human experience, which is a problem since human intervention taints objectivity. In short, Peirce and Saussure's theories ignore, or bracket, the question of how signs incorporate an objective world. The focus is not on what exists but on what people think exists.

Consider again, Barthes's study of food fantasy, and Seiter's study of children of color in magazine images. These critics, for the most part, emphasize people's belief systems or social realities. Barthes attends to how the food images psychologically and socially satisfy a group of people. Seiter attends to how the images of children create a psychological and social reality. Seiter does, however, move out of the semiological system when she claims that "in fact" most people who live in poverty are white.

The point that traditional semiotics does not account for the material world in meaning is viewed as a problem by some thinkers but as an opportunity for others to critique, extend, alter, and combine the ideas of Saussure and Peirce. The displacement of the material world in semiotic theories of meaning is particularly appealing to the contemporary-postmodern philosophy that humans only know reality through communication about reality (Gottdiener, pp. 19-25). The result, for critics, is a plethora of semiotic approaches that are valuable for unraveling the ways signifiers shape our ideas and identities.

 Note

1. The following sources provide introductory discussions of semiotics: Belsey (1980); Fiske and Hartley, (1984); Hawkes (1977); and Seiter (1987).

5 Language as Metaphor

The metaphoric perspective, a third way to view language critically, is not distinct from the stylistic or semiotic perspectives. Metaphor was, in fact, defined within the discussion of style as a figure of speech that states or implies that two things are the same. It is with metaphor that politicians have addressed the Soviet Union as a grizzly bear. The metaphor is also captured in the semiotic framework. All signifiers—not just words—are potential metaphors. It is a metaphorical process when a child signifies innocence or a cartoon image signifies the president. According to Fiske and Hartley (1984), metaphors and signs involve the "transposition or displacement from signified to signifier, together with the recognition that such a transposition implies an equivalence between these two elements of the sign" (p. 48).

Similar to semiotics, metaphors capture language and meaning in thought. George Lakoff and Mark Johnson's *Metaphors We Live By* (1980) makes a convincing case that metaphors organize how we think. Like others who study metaphor, they identify metaphors as a cognitive or intellectual process. It is through the metaphor of laissez-faire economics, for instance, that Charles Darwin is said to have invented the theory of evolution. The metaphor, a process of moving from one idea to another, is how people invent or discover ideas (Ivie, 1987/1995). Ideas and ideologies are invented and maintained in metaphors. For instance, Edwin Black (1970/1995) unravels the ideology in "communism is a cancer" metaphors that were common among right-wing politicians during the cold war. He outlines the "ideas" Americans had about cancer that were transferred to ideas about communism: Cancer invades (a war metaphor itself) from within one's body; cancer grows, spreads, and corrupts; cancer is a punishment for immoral behavior; cancer is terrifying; cancer is incurable, eventually resulting in death.

Metaphors are also viewed as having reference to human experience and the physical universe. Metaphors found across cultures and time refer to universal experiences such as childbirth, death, or the sunrise. Lakoff and Johnson claim metaphors are not arbitrary in their reference but are rooted in cultural and sometimes physical experiences. Orientation metaphors may arise from "the fact that we have bodies of the sort we have and that they function as they do in our physical environment" (p. 14). For instance, people often speak of health in terms of "up" and "down": "He is in the *peak* of health"; "he is in *top* shape"; "his health is *declining*," or "he *dropped* dead." The physical origins of the "health is up" and "sick is down" may be that when we are ill we lie down.

Other than being rooted in nature or human experience in nature, metaphors actually give shape to our perceptions, conceptions, and even behaviors. In the case of metaphors that equate cancer and communism, one might risk one's own life to stop the spread of cancer and do the same to stop communism. In other examples, Susan Sontag's *AIDS and its Metaphors* (1989) and her earlier *Illness as Metaphor* (1979) elucidate the ways patients become helpless "victims" of illnesses, or rather the metaphors of illness. Emily Martin (1987) shows how the metaphors used to discuss menstruation and menopause in medical and popular texts contribute to, if not create, them as negative experiences. She identifies a plethora of contemporary metaphors that construct the woman's body as a machine and menstruation as a failure of the machine to produce a baby: "The fall" of blood "deprives" the endometrial lining of its hormonal support; "constriction" of blood vessels leads to a "diminished" supply of oxygen and nutrients; the blood vessels undergo "spasms"; "deteriorating" tissue is "discharged" as menstrual flow. Menopause is a total breakdown or deterioration of the machine: The ovaries "regress"; because of the "withdrawal" of estrogen, the hypothalamus "gives inappropriate orders"; the pituitary gland becomes "disturbed" when the ovaries "fail" to respond. The ideologies of metaphors may become our realities.

We have seen many similarities between metaphoric views of language and stylistic and semiotic views. The metaphor's distinctiveness is found in its vocabulary—its way of directing and deflecting the critic's attention. Thinking critically about metaphors is not usually as precise as dissecting signifiers or as intangible as considering the qualities of style. The conceptual vocabulary for a critical reading of metaphors includes analyzing the parts of a metaphor, as well as considering a wide variety of metaphoric relations. Overall, the concept of "transformation" is a useful way to describe how metaphors make meaning, because it captures the idea of something actually becoming something else.

Metaphoric Transformations

Because people frequently, if not always, think and communicate in metaphors, we often fail to recognize them as metaphors. Familiarizing yourself with the vocabulary of metaphoric relations is the first step to sharpening your critical awareness of metaphoric meaning. Once recognized, the critic moves to the systematic process of thinking about the parts of a metaphor and their transformations.

The metaphoric relations that have been uncovered are varied and many. Only a few of these relations will be considered here to help us see the metaphors that surround us. Some metaphors transform objects into people and vice versa. Lakoff and Johnson (1980) label these ontological metaphors and define them as "ways of viewing events, activities, emotions, ideas, etc., as entities and substances . . . "(p. 25) and to "comprehend a wide variety of experiences with nonhuman entities in terms of human motivations, characteristics, and activities" (p.33). The following are some examples of ontological metaphors: "Inflation backs us into a corner," "We have to deal with inflation," "My mind has shut down for the day," and "My heart is broken." The two parts of a metaphor may share a literal or imaginative relationship. Some metaphors are metonymies, which are metaphors of association. The association of part to whole, or synecdoche, is a familiar metonymy. Metonymies are referential metaphors, as when a filmmaker uses an image of the Statue of Liberty in reference to New York or the United States.

Tenor-Vehicle

Critics have found the philosopher I. A. Richards's proposed means of capturing metaphors useful. Metaphors, according to Richards, join tenor and vehicle. The tenor of a metaphor is the subject being addressed. The Soviet Union is a tenor in Ronald Reagan's "bear in the woods" campaign advertisement. The vehicle for thinking about the Soviet Union includes the systems of meaning embodied in our experiences and beliefs about bears. Similarly, cancer patients are the tenor and victimage is the vehicle in metaphors that cast illness as the weapon of our supernatural enemies.

Tenor and vehicle meet in metaphor as signifier meets signified in sign. The difference between the metaphoric and semiotic perspective on meaning is that the vehicle of a metaphor is a system of thought, whereas the signifier is not necessarily imbued with meaning. In other words, the concept of vehicle-tenor transforms meaning, whereas signifiers assume—at least theoretically—a point of meaninglessness. As a signifier in his advertising campaigns, Reagan's bear is an image. The signifier takes on meaning insofar as it looks like a bear, is an index of danger, and symbolizes the Soviet Union. The image of the bear takes on ideological meanings at the second and third orders of relationships where it meets and participates in systems of meaning about bears, the Soviet Union, communism, and democracy. As a metaphor, Reagan's bear is the transformation of these systems of meaning. There is a very clear critical starting point in the audience's beliefs relevant to bears.

Clusters

Metaphors that are repeated by individuals, cultures, or both, reveal much about the individual or collective consciousness. If we encounter one or two metaphors that equate menopause with deterioration, we would not want to generalize that it is the way menopause is viewed or experienced. However, when particular metaphors become a common pattern in communication, as has menopause deterioration, they do suggest a dominant view of menopause. A critic exploring metaphoric recurrences or any repetitious linguistic or semiological patterns, would need to study samples of communication texts that represent the speaker or culture. The communication texts may be selected, or narrowed, on the basis of subject matter, as well. For her study of how Americans experience menstruation and menopause, for instance, Martin studied popular science textbooks and influential scientific reports that address women's physiology.

The critic then moves systematically through the texts, identifying **clusters of metaphoric vehicles** that carry a common tenor.[1] For instance, Jane Blankenship (1980) identified clusters of vehicles for describing political campaigns in American newspapers to include "violence," "sports," and "war." The critic probes deeper into metaphoric relations by identifying clusters within the metaphoric clusters. For example, sports metaphors are further clustered into baseball, swimming, and wrestling. The critic interested in ideologies, or belief systems, explores the relationships within and between clusters. Violence, sports, and war share winners and losers. The sports metaphors share spectators cheering, jeering, and wanting an exciting game. The belief system entailed in this clustering of metaphors is that politics is about action, not issues; the public should watch politics, rather than participate in politics; and campaigns are ultimately about who will win, not how we can improve society. Blankenship's study of metaphors in campaigns was conducted many years ago. The violence, sports, and war metaphors, and their implied ideology, seem just as prevalent today.

▓▓ Critical Questions and Answers

Again, let us summarize the critical study of metaphors through some overall questions that critics have asked and answered. Because all language can be viewed as metaphor, it is often difficult to recognize the tree in the forest. Once the communication text(s), metaphor(s), and context(s) are identified, the critic finds meaning in how the audience will transform vehicle into tenor and perhaps cluster vehicles into tenors. Though the sample studies that follow focus on words, metaphors can encompass a wide range of vehicles.

1. Does the use of metaphor fulfill the speaker's purpose? Explain.

Critical comment on effectiveness: Martha Solomon (1985/1994) considers how metaphors were used effectively in the research reports on the Tuskegee Syphilis Project. The Tuskegee study, now considered unethical, followed untreated syphilis in black men for a period of 40 years (beginning in 1932). One hundred men died in the name of the scientific knowledge that was supposedly gained from this study. Solomon illustrates how the scientific reports effectively justified and maintained the study by referring to the "men" studied as tenor to the vehicle "scene" or "host" of the disease. These metaphors worked because they depersonalized the men in the study. They created "detachment from the content being discussed," so that human emotion is tempered in favor of objective, scientific knowing.

2. Is the metaphor used truthfully and ethically?

Critical comment on truth and ethics: By depersonalizing the men in the study, the Tuskegee reports distorted "our vision and obscured the salient features of reality" (Solomon, p. 316). Solomon concludes that, if the language of the Tuskegee reports "blinds us to other values, it produces neither humane behavior nor science" (p. 320).

3. How does the use of metaphor shape identities, ideas, and actions?

Critical comment on identities, ideas, and actions: Susan Sontag's (1989) study of contemporary AIDS metaphors illustrates how the "military" and "plagues" are systematically used as vehicles for the tenor "AIDS." The war metaphor assumes several beliefs: The virus that causes AIDS "invades," and as the immune system is "alerted" to the presence of a "foreigner" it "mobilizes" cells to deal with the "threat" (p.17). As a plague, and as war, the enemy virus comes from outside, never inside—the creation of others, never ourselves (p. 47). In both instances, the metaphors shape an identity of the AIDS patient as a victim. Sontag explains that, although AIDS is a war and patients are victims, the metaphor does not assume the victims are innocent, only helpless (p. 11).

The metaphoric approach to language has its strengths and weaknesses as an interpretive tool. As was previously mentioned, it has a clear critical starting point at the beliefs entailed in the metaphoric vehicle. It is not necessarily as tedious as semiotics. It is also better suited to the study of some forms of communication. For instance, the metaphoric perspective can capture the richness and resonance of Martin Luther King's speaking more than can the semiotic perspective. The study of metaphors, similar to the study of style and sign systems, is not always critically insightful. The final questions that should be asked from within any perspective are (a) Does the perspective give us a better understanding of communication? And (b) Does the perspective lead us to a decision about who we are, what we should believe, and how we should act?

I believe the studies by Sontag and Solomon reveal the power of language in creating our reality. The metaphors found in "objective" scientific reports clearly function as terministic screens for our reality.

The Tuskegee and AIDS reports hail identities for African American men, people with AIDS, and doctors-scientists. The metaphors determined the physical existence for the African American men in the study (and influence the socioeconomic position of African Americans today) and for all people "living" with AIDS. Even when Solomon is interested in the effectiveness of the reports, in gaining continued government funding she reveals ideologies. Aside from an ideology that renders African Americans as nonhuman and doctors-scientists as superhuman, Solomon shows us how the language in the Tuskegee reports reinforces our culture's ideology of knowledge: True knowledge is scientific, objective, and most valuable; we can justify almost any act that advances scientific knowledge. Sontag and Solomon make convincing cases that metaphors influence human behavior.

Note

1. The method of clustering metaphors that is described here is based on Robert Ivie's (1987/1995) discussion of metaphor as a process of rhetorical invention.

Reference List For Unit II

Allan, L. (1939). Strange fruit [recorded by B. Holiday]. On [unknown record]. New York: PolyGram Records, Inc.
Aristotle (1954). *Rhetoric*. (W. Rhys Roberts, Trans.). New York: Random House.
Arnold, C. C. (1974). *Criticism of oral rhetoric*. Columbus, OH: Charles E. Merrill.
Barthes, R. (1980). *Mythologies*. (A. Lavers, Trans.). New York: Hill & Wang.
Belsey, C. (1980). *Critical practice*. New York: Methuen.
Black, E. (1970). The second persona. *Quarterly Journal of Speech, 56*, 109-119.
Blair, H. D. (1965). *Letters on rhetoric and belles lettres*. (H. F. Harding, Ed.) Carbondale: Southern Illinois University Press.
Blankenship, J. (1968). *A sense of style*. Belmont, CA: Dickenson Publishing.
Blankenship, J. (1980). The search for the 1972 democratic nomination: A metaphorical perspective. In R. L. Scott, & B. L. Brock (Eds.), *Methods of rhetorical criticism: A twentieth-century perspective* (2nd ed.). Detroit, MI: Wayne State University Press.
Bowers, D. L. (1994). Afrocentrism and *Do the right thing*. In B. Brummett (Ed.), *Rhetoric in popular culture* (pp. 199-221). New York: St. Martin's.
Buchanan, P. (1992). The election is about who we are (speech). *Vital Speeches of the Day, 52*, 712-717.

Burke, K. (1966). *Language as symbolic action.* Berkeley: University of California Press.

Campbell, K. K. (1972). An exercise in the rhetoric of mythical America. In K. K. Campbell, *Critiques of contemporary rhetoric* (pp. 50-58). Belmont, CA: Wadsworth.

Cicero (1949) *De oratore.* (E. W. Sutton, & H. Rackham, Trans.) Cambridge, MA: Harvard University Press.

Fiske J., & Hartley, J. (1984). *Reading television.* New York: Methuen.

Foss, S. K. (1989). *Rhetorical criticism: Exploration and practice.* Prospect Heights, IL: Waveland Press.

Golden, J. L., Berquist, G. F., & Coleman, W. E. (1992). *The rhetoric of western thought* (5th ed.). Dubuque, IA: Kendall/Hunt.

Gottdiener, M. (1995). *Postmodern semiotics: Material culture and the forms of postmodern life.* Cambridge, MA: Blackwell.

Grassi, E. (1980). *Rhetoric as philosophy.* University Park: Pennsylvania State University Press.

Hawkes, T. (1977). *Structuralism and semiotics.* London: Methuen.

Hill, F. (1990). Conventional wisdom—traditional form—The President's message of November 3, 1969. In J. R. Andrews (Ed.), *The Practice of rhetorical criticism* (pp. 127-140). New York: Longman. (Reprinted from Speech Communication Association, 1972)

Holiday, B. [ref. Allan, L.]

Ivie, R.L. (1995). Metaphor and the rhetorical invention of cold war idealists. In C. R. Burgchardt (Ed.), *Readings in rhetorical criticism* (pp. 347-364). State College, PA: Strata Publishing. (Reprinted from *Communication Monographs, 54,* 1987)

Jackson, J. (1984). The rainbow coalition (speech). In J. R. Andrews, & D. Zarefsky (Eds.), *Contemporary American voices* (pp. 355-362). White Plains, NY: Longman.

Kane, K. (1990). The ideology of freshness in feminine hygiene commercials. *Journal of Communication Inquiry, 14,* 82-92.

King, M. L. (1963). I have a dream (speech). In J. R. Andrews, & D. Zarefsky (Eds.), *Contemporary American voices* (pp. 78-81). White Plains, NY: Longman.

Lakoff, G., & Johnson, M. (1980). *Metaphors we live by.* Chicago: University of Chicago Press.

Leff, M. (1995). Dimensions of temporality in Lincoln's Second Inaugural. In C. R. Burgchardt (Ed.), *Readings in rhetorical criticism* (pp. 526-531). State College, PA: Strata Publishing. (Reprinted from *Communication Reports, 1,* 1988)

Lule, J. (1995). The rape of Mike Tyson: Race, the press and symbolic types. *Critical Studies in Mass Communication, 12,* 176-195.

Martin, E. (1987). *The woman in the body.* Boston: Beacon.

Nixon, R. M. (1952). Checkers (speech). In J. R. Andrews, & D. Zarefsky (Eds.), *Contemporary American voices* (pp. 41-48). White Plains, NY: Longman.

Nixon, R. M. (1969). Vietnamization (speech). In J. R. Andrews, & D. Zarefsky (Eds.), *Contemporary American voices* (pp. 240-248). White Plains, NY: Longman.

Peirce, C. S. (1931-1935). In P. Weiss, & C. Harthshone (Eds.), *Collected papers.* Cambridge, MA: Harvard University Press.

Reagan R. (1984). Television campaign advertisement for the 1984 presidential election. On *The classics of political television advertising* [video]. Aurora, CO: Meyer Communications.

Richards, I. A. (1965). *The philosophy of rhetoric.* New York: Galaxy.

Saussure, F. (1974). *Course in general linguistics.* (W. Baskin, Trans.). London: Fontana.

Seiter, E. (1987). Semiotics and television. In R. C. Allen (Ed.), *Channels of discourse* (pp. 17-41). Chapel Hill, NC: University.

Seiter, E. (1990). Different children, different dreams: Racial representation in advertising. *Journal of Communication Inquiry, 14,* 31-47.

Solomon, M. (1978). Jimmy Carter and *Playboy*: A sociolinguistic perspective on style. *The Quarterly Journal of Speech, 64,* 173-182.

Solomon, M. (1994). The rhetoric of dehumanization: An analysis of medical reports of the Tuskegee Syphilis Project. In W. Nothstine, C. Blair, & G. Copeland (Eds.), *Critical questions: Invention, creativity, and the criticism of discourse and media* (pp. 301-322). New York: St. Martin's. (Reprinted from *Western Journal of Speech Communication, 49,* 1985, pp. 233-247)

Sontag, S. (1979). *Illness as metaphor.* New York: Vintage.

Sontag, S. (1989). *AIDS and its metaphors.* New York: Farrar, Straus, & Giroux.

Stewart, J. R. (1972). Concepts of language and meaning: A comparative study. *The Quarterly Journal of Speech, 58,* 122-133.

Taylor, E. (1990). Statement to the Task Force on Human Resources (speech). In V. L. Defrancisco, & M. D. Jensen (Eds.), *Women's voices in our time: Statements by American leaders* (pp. 69-74). Prospect Heights, IL: Waveland Press.

Thonssen, L., Baird, A. G., & Braden, W. W. (1970). *Speech criticism* (2nd ed.). New York: Ronald Press.

Tuchman, G., & Levine, H. G. (1993). New York Jews and Chinese food: The social construction of an ethnic pattern. *Journal of Contemporary Ethnography, 22,* 382-402.

Wattleton, F. (1991). Address at the triennial convention of the YWCA (speech). In V. L. Defrancisco, & M. D. Jensen (Eds.), *Women's voices in our time: Statements by American leaders* (pp. 129-136). Prospect Heights, IL: Waveland Press.

UNIT III

CRITICAL CONCEPTS THAT
FOCUS ON STRUCTURE

We are creatures of order. We sequence our collective lives into decades, centuries, and epochs. We divide our days into parts, whether they be "morning, afternoon, evening" or "work time and free time." When you were just a child, you probably thought about your life in terms of years or school grades. As life goes on, you reorder it into key events, relationships, or the places where you have lived. A popular book in the 1970s, *Passages* (Sheehy) lays out the five stages of life: The *New Passages* (1996) adds a sixth stage to account for the increased longevity of people's lives by adding a second career passage to the structure of middle-class American life.

We order our belongings, too. You may remember yourself as a child arranging the Halloween goodies you collected into groups of "chocolate and all others," "most favorite to least favorite," or by name brands. We arrange our clothing in closets, dressers, on shelves, and/or in boxes according to clothing items. Some of us further arrange our clothes by season. And many of us have a special place for those things that do not seem to fit into our organizational scheme.

The words *ordering, organizing,* and *arranging* are used here synony-
mously with *structuring,* as in the title of this unit. They all describe
the process of dividing or drawing boundaries around ideas and things
and establishing relationships among them. This unit will deal with
the ways we structure language, whether language consists of words,
metaphors, or all signifiers.

If one is to think about how the structure of communication
becomes meaningful, one must think through the structure of the
language because the components of meaning are interdependent.
Rhetorical form is a term that brings language and structure together.
Form, according to literary critic, theorist, and novelist, Kenneth
Burke (1968) is the "creation of an appetite in the mind of the auditor,
and the adequate satisfying of that appetite" (p. 31). It is a concept
that also links the psychology of the audience with the text. Style,
particularly the methods of amplification, arouse and satisfy the
expectations of an audience. When we hear the beginning of an
antithesis such as, "ask not what your country can do for you," we
anticipate the conclusion of the stylistic form, "but ask what you can
do for your country." Structure arouses expectations in a similar way.
If we meet for dinner and you ask, "How was your day?" I may
respond in chronological order: "Well, first I woke up late and missed
the bus. When I finally got to work, things went OK, but at lunch I
ran into my old boss and. . . ." The time-pattern of my speech should
arouse your expectation that my monologue will continue to describe
the day in a chronological pattern.

It is impossible to use language without it falling into some sort of
pattern. All symbolic action, not just words, creates form. Our dinner
date, for example, will follow a pattern of expected symbolic actions
from the waiter bringing the menu to paying the check at the end of
the meal. Your asking about my day is part of conversational form.
When Burke explains the idea of form he distinguishes between form
in the small and form in the large (1969b, pp. 65-78). Stylistic
considerations fall into the former category; the structural patterns
discussed in this chapter tend to fall into the latter category. These
distinctions are quite abstract and do not offer the beginning critic
many guidelines; therefore, this unit presents some other avenues for

thinking critically about structure, and all of them can be considered as form.

More specifically, this unit will consider four ways critics frame the structure of communication. We begin once again with the theories of classical rhetoric. **Organization,** or *dispositio* as ancient rhetoricians called it, emphasizes how the arrangement of ideas in speech shapes beliefs and behaviors. The second concept, **editing,** describes how film and video images are structured into meaning. The third and fourth concepts, **narrative** and **drama,** view structure in communication as the order we give to our lives. The four concepts, used separately or in combination, can be applied to a wide range of symbolic communication from rituals to everyday talk. In every case, language, which comes in many forms, is the vehicle for structuring.

6 Structure as Organization

The neo-Aristotelian theory of structure offers speakers some basic rules for expressing ideas clearly and persuasively. Practical communication books from Aristotle's *Rhetoric* (Book III, Chaps. 13 & 14) to any contemporary public-speaking textbook agree that organized speech includes themes, central ideas, main ideas, transitions, and organizational patterns. This very practical theory of organization can be used to think critically about speech and a variety of other communication forms.

For example, President Franklin D. Roosevelt organized his speech in support of the Lend-Lease bill (1941) to motivate his audience to action. The Lend-Lease Act allowed the president to give necessary supplies to those countries fighting for democracy in World War II. In the first part of the speech, Roosevelt establishes freedom as a common ground between himself and the audience. He then introduces the threat to democratic freedom and his plan to deter the threat through the Lend-Lease bill. He appeals to Americans to support the bill in spirit but also calls for them to "move products from the assembly lines of our factories to the battle lines of democracy—now!" Bruce Springsteen, the musical artist who rose to fame in the 1980s, may not have been calling his audience to social action, but the structure of his music is critically interesting. According to Michael McGuire (1984), the relationship among key themes in Springsteen's lyrics expresses the identity of the speaker and invites the audience to identify a similar view of reality. The vocabulary of organization also guided a critical study of feminist-artist Judy Chicago's installation artwork entitled, *The Dinner Party* (Foss, 1988/1996). The so-called text of *The Dinner Party* is an actual table, with settings for 39 historical women. Foss explains how the public display of female themes legitimizes women's identity and may "suggest new options for the viewers in their own lives" (p. 218). Although organization is a concept that originated as a theory of how to structure speech, it can be adapted to thinking critically about most communication. As a critical concept, organization can help us to understand our actions, ideas, and even identities.

▨ Parts and Principles of Organization

Before a critic can use the traditional concept of organization in insightful ways, he or she must know the basic principles for arranging ideas in verbal communication. They should seem familiar, as it is likely teachers have been instructing you to follow these principles for many years. The principles are prescriptive, that is, they suggest how communication should be organized. We begin here with the broader concepts, themes and theses, and move into the specific ways they are structured into speech and writing.

Themes and Theses

Speeches, magazine articles, advertising campaigns, news reports, and novels include a controlling theme if not a thesis. Much more general than a thesis, a **theme** can be expressed in a word or a phrase. A theme would be "illegal drug use" or "drugs and crime." A thesis is a declarative sentence: "As the use of illegal drugs increases, so does crime." Themes are easy to come by, they even emerge in spontaneous conversations. Comedians, television shows, and films obviously have themes. Themes are typically conveyed through stylistic emphasis, often through repetition. Campaign speeches carry an endorsement theme. Advertisements for Calvin Klein jeans (1995) have a sexuality theme. The comedian Jerry Seinfeld tends to address interpersonal relationship themes. News stories about Africa often carry a hunger theme. Themes pose some interesting critical questions, such as, what themes did a speaker choose to develop, why, and with what effects? I will return to these questions. For now, let us consider other concepts related to the organization of communication.

A **thesis,** also called a **central idea,** is found in communication that is purposeful. Speakers and writers who intend to persuade or inform an audience typically have a point, called a thesis, and they design their communication around the thesis. The thesis is more specific and focused than the theme and can therefore be stated as a full, direct sentence. The potential theses for any given theme are limitless. Each of the following statements, for instance, is an appropriate thesis on the theme of drug abuse: Illegal drug use is cultural; the tendency for people to abuse drugs is physiological; legalizing drugs will reduce drug use and crime; just say no to illegal drug use; some illegal drugs may have medicinal value.

A speaker might explicitly state or imply a thesis. Speakers who intend to inform, as teachers do, usually state their thesis at the beginning of their talk. Speakers who open with a thesis allow their audiences to focus on the most relevant ideas as they speak. An introductory thesis is important to most informational communication because it provides the audience with a system for processing and remembering the information. In persuasive talk, the thesis may offend the audience and so speakers will often establish some common ground with the audience before revealing their overall point. The Church of Latter Day Saints has been airing an antiabortion television campaign that establishes common ground with the audience through a series of photographs of children laughing and playing. The topic (abortion) or thesis (stop abortion) are not revealed until the conclusion of the spot. The placement of the thesis at the end of the message allows the church to more effectively move the audience to its position before revealing its stance.

Effective communicators understand the value of a thesis and will use it to arrange all of their ideas. An insightful critic of communication considers the thesis even when speakers lack one or fail to make it clear. Being creatures of order, audiences will often impose a thesis on messages that do not seem to have one. In word or image, explicit or implicit, intentional or not, a thesis is the essence of a communication text. A thesis summarizes the substance of an hour of talk, 20 pages of writing, or 30 minutes of video in one sentence.

Boundaries and Relationships

The thesis is a whole containing parts. The parts of a thesis are its **main ideas**, which can be further divided into **subordinate ideas**. Main ideas divide the thesis into somewhat equal territories. For instance, the thesis "I had a miserable day" could be addressed in two parts: "at work" and "after work." The thesis "This health plan has three problems" would likely contain three main ideas. The boundaries of the main ideas are marked by their relationship to one another. Communication is believed to be well-organized when these ideas are related to one another in standard ways called organizational patterns. People relate ideas in a variety of ways, and some cultures favor some organizational patterns over others. Here are some organizational patterns commonly used in American culture:

Main ideas related in time:
Thesis: I had a miserable day.

1. My work day was a disaster.
2. After work, things got worse.
3. The evening brought on one crisis after another.

Main ideas related in space:
Thesis: The university is a complex organization.

1. The board of trustees oversees all major decisions at the university.
2. The office of the President works with the board and can veto its decisions.
3. The administrators include a hierarchy of offices that coordinate decisions regarding curricular, co-curricular, and financial issues.
4. The faculty and staff, representing a variety of departments, participate in some of the decision-making processes.
5. Students have the power to influence all the levels of decision making in the university.

Main ideas related through cause and effect:
Thesis: Building the new mall will hurt local businesses.

1. The proposed shopping mall will offer a variety of goods and services to residents.
2. Local businesses will be unable to compete with the mall.

Main ideas related through comparison-contrast:
Thesis: Small colleges offer a different atmosphere for learning than do larger universities.

1. Small colleges often provide a more intimate learning situation through smaller student-teacher ratios.
2. What larger universities may lack in instruction they make up for in the availability of co-curricular activities.

Main ideas related through problem-solution:
Thesis: Recycling can help to reduce garbage.

1. Human beings create an amazing amount of garbage.
2. The process of recycling can alleviate the problems created by waste.

Main ideas related by topic:
Thesis: Small colleges have many advantages over larger universities.

1. The student-teacher ratio is smaller at colleges.
2. Smaller colleges often have a community atmosphere.
3. Students often have a greater role in decision making at smaller colleges.

Main ideas related hierarchically:
Thesis: I had a miserable day.

1. I was late for work and several appointments during the day.
2. I learned my bank account was overdrawn.
3. I crashed my car into a tree.
4. My dog died.

Main ideas, similar to chapters and acts within a play, may be further divided into subordinate parts. Subordinate ideas elaborate on, clarify, and support main ideas. They also can form a relationship to one another. Consider our topical thesis above as an example. While the main ideas may be related topically, the subordinate ideas may be related by comparison-contrast:

Thesis: Small colleges have many advantages over larger universities.

1. The student-teacher ratio is smaller at colleges.
   a. Teachers at the small college can get to know students and their learning styles.

    b. At universities, large classes and research-oriented professors put a greater burden on the student to get to know their teachers.

2. Smaller colleges have a community atmosphere.

    a. Less student enrollment means it's easier to participate in co-curricular activities and to get to know other students on campus.

    b. The enrollment at large universities makes involvement in co-curricular activities more competitive.

3. Students can have a greater role in decision making at small colleges.

    a. In small colleges, increased interaction among students, teachers, and administrators allows students more influence in the policy-making process.

    b. Though large universities offer students formal channels of influence and participation, their students typically perceive low involvement in decision making.

In short, people articulate ideas at various levels of abstraction. We have discussed three layers of ideas: theses, main ideas, and subordinate ideas. **Transitional** statements between key ideas should clarify and reinforce the pattern of speech for the audience. The layers of ideas unfold within the **body** of a speech, conversation, or written document. Typically the body of ideas is placed between an **introduction** and a **conclusion**. Even a telephone conversation involves greetings and closings. An effective introduction will establish a positive connection between the speaker/writer and the audience, gain the audience's attention, and make the topic, the thesis, or both relevant to the interests of the audience. The introduction may or may not state the thesis and preview the main ideas, depending on the speaker/writer's strategy. The conclusion often summarizes the main ideas and thesis but on occasion will serve as a climax of communication by revealing the, as yet, unstated thesis.

A critic uses this vocabulary of parts and principles of organization to map out communication. If well organized, the ideas and their relationships suggest a thesis on a given topic. In general, well-organized communication will also arouse and fulfill the audience's expectations. There are circumstances when speakers violate expected patterns for good reasons. A speaker may want the audience to conceive of an idea in a new way or to emerge from a communication text more agitated than fulfilled.

Critical interpretation involves more than outlining and deciding whether the communication is well organized, it is understanding how

place and **space** will effect meaning. For example, a critical study of newspaper stories about boxing champion Mike Tyson's rape trial notes that most papers placed the trial stories in the sports section, possibly trivializing the severity of the alleged crime (Lule, 1995). The critical study of *The Dinner Party,* noted at the outset of this chapter, claims that one of the reasons the work of art empowers women is that it refuses to include a space for men. It refuses men space in the obvious form of a seat at the historical table, but it also ignores male images and art forms, thereby presenting women as legitimate in their own right (Foss, 1988/ 1996).

As a way of reviewing the basic principles of organization, examine the following outline of Wilma P. Mankiller's (1991/1994) second Inaugural Address as Principle Chief of the Cherokee Nation. It is a well-organized speech as prescribed by the ancient Greek theorists and reinforced through 2,500 years of Western thought.

Introduction: Greetings and thanks to the Tribal Council and citizens of the Cherokee Nation for your support.

Thesis: The Cherokee Nation has been maintained through a history of adversity, and we must continue to keep the voice of the Cherokee alive.

1. For more than two centuries, we have survived attempts to abolish the Cherokee Nation.
   a. At the turn of the 19th century, we fought for our sovereignty.
      (1) removal of people from their homeland
      (2) U.S. government promises independence for land
   b. At the turn of the 20th century, our tribal government was diminished.
      (1) Oklahoma became a state and closed our schools, our tribal judicial system
      (2) common land was divided into individual allotments
      (3) Cherokee chiefs were appointed by the U.S. government
   c. In the last 20 years, we have revitalized the Cherokee Nation.
      (1) financial gains
      (2) social gains
2. It is up to us to honor our ancestors and their work by keeping the Cherokee Nation healthy into the 21st Century.
   a. We have many problems.
      (1) education

(2) health care crisis
(3) poverty
b. In the next few years, let us actively address these problems.
(1) get involved in the community
(2) do even more than we've been doing

Conclusion: Thanks again to family, friends, and the Cherokee Nation for your support. And congratulations to the Cherokee Council for your excellent work over the last term.[1]

The organization of speech, or any form of communication, should enable its audience to understand and remember what is being said. But organization also functions as a terministic screen, revealing some ideas and concealing others. A useful means of uncovering the ways structure shapes meaning is to consider alternative ways a particular piece of communication could be organized and how its meaning would change. More specifically, consider alternatives to how the ideas are placed, as well as how much space is dedicated to each idea. For instance, had Mankiller first talked about the future and then the past, the audience might have received a more pessimistic meaning. Had she organized her ideas into a cause-and-effect pattern, the speech would have emphasized those who are to blame for the Cherokee's struggle. The speech might have been antagonistic if she had not spent relatively equal time on the future as she did on the past.

Critical Questions and Answers

We can convert the principles of how to organize communication into questions for thinking critically about how organization shapes our realities. I have selected to paraphrase parts of a critical essay by Richard Fulkerson (1979/1984) as an illustration of how one critic uses the concept. Fulkerson uses the neo-Aristotelian approach to structure to evaluate the effectiveness of a letter Martin Luther King wrote to the public. Fulkerson determines King's purpose through a study of the letter itself and the context of its creation and publication in 1963. He then considers how King directed his audiences to believe civil protest is an acceptable political act through the arrangement of his ideas.

1. **Does the organization of the communication effectively inform and/or persuade the intended audience? Explain.**

Critical comment on effectiveness: Richard Fulkerson illustrates how Martin Luther King's "Letter from Birmingham Jail" is organized persuasively. The letter, written by King after his 1963 arrest for civil disobedience, responds to a public letter, signed by eight clergymen and printed in the *Birmingham News.* The clergymen's letter asked civil rights protesters to work through the court system instead of partaking in civil disobedience. King's letter fulfilled his purpose, to persuade the general public and his less committed supporters that the clergymen were incorrect and that social protest was the right action to take.

King made his thesis, "the white power structure of this city left the Negro community with no other alternative," clear by addressing six issues that were initially raised by the clergymen. King does not address the issues in the same order as the clergymen; rather, he "wisely adapts the order of his main arguments to move from the obvious to the more complex, presumably for the benefit of the wider audience" (p. 300).

Twice during the speech, King seemingly digresses from this pattern to talk about his personal feelings about the response of the wider, white, liberal community to the protests. The personal digressions, obvious breaks from his argumentative pattern, suggest King is being spontaneous, and they allow "King to attack without seeming aggressive" (p. 301).

2. **Does the organization of the communication text present the world, ideas about the world, or both, truthfully and ethically? Explain.**

Critical comment on truth and ethics: Because King structures his refutation of the clergymen's case against civil protest in such a clear, precise way, his readers will believe "a man who can perform these tasks is able and honest and worthy of belief" (Fulkerson, p. 305).

King's letter is "both readable and thorough. Its refutative stance makes it alive with the fire of heated but courteous controversy, and the dual nature of the refutation makes it simultaneously persuasive and logically compelling" (Fulkerson, p. 312).

3. **How does the organization of the text shape identities, ideas, and actions?**

Critical comment on identities, ideas, and actions: King was able to gain adherence to his belief that civil protest is the right action through the organization of his letter. He first addresses the clergymen's claim that negotiation is better than a sit-in or a public march. He agrees with them and in so doing, "King logically and gracefully turns the argument back on the clergymen: Certainly negotiation is desirable; the *goal* of the protest is precisely to make the other side willing to negotiate" (Fulkerson, p. 300).

Fulkerson's study illustrates the usefulness of using organization as a critical tool. By studying the strategies of those we have come to think of as master communicators such as King, we learn ways of persuading and being persuaded through the arrangement of ideas. Fulkerson, like any critic thinking in terms of structure, attends to how ideas are related, connected, synthesized, and transformed. To study the boundaries and relationships among ideas in communication is to study the ideologies of culture. For instance, the boundaries King created in his refutative structure appealed to different ideologies. King's overall refutative structure addresses politically moderate, Southern, white, religious leaders. Within the refutation, he hails a wider audience of white, liberal, opinion leaders, uncommitted to civil rights. King's words also draw boundaries around alternative social actions: either negotiation or civil protest.

Insights into cultural identities and ideologies invite judgments of ethics and truthfulness. We do not usually think of the organization of speech as being truthful. But the structure of speech, as we have seen, maps out potential identities and ideologies; therefore questions of ethics are often relevant. Is the speaker's purpose ethical? Is the speaker's thesis ethical? What kinds of actions may result?

Considered within the framework of organization, truthfulness is often a question of whether the structure was convincing. Fulkerson addresses truthfulness in this way, claiming King's structure moved the audience to believe an idea is true and that the speaker is truthful.

The limitations of using organization as a guide are that it is prescriptive and presents a rather linear way of thinking about structure. The critic should remember that the principles of organization identified here are not always appropriate. Different cultures, contexts, and communication texts are always establishing new patterns/forms of communication. However, the themes of traditional organization run through all approaches to structure. The next few chapters present alternative forms for viewing structure. Most of them employ some of the vocabulary of organization.

 Note

1. I outlined Chief Mankiller's speech from a text of the speech printed in V. Defrancisco and M. Jensen's (1994) *Women's Voices in our Time.*

7 Structure as Editing Images

Video- and filmmakers have developed a vocabulary for understanding the structure of how images shape meaning. **Editing** is the general name given to the process of arranging images, and it is the concept we will use to think about the arrangement of images. Learning about editing can present an entirely new way to see television and film. For many, learning the vocabulary of editing is initially disheartening for it can take some of the magic out of going to the movies. But a critical view of editing reveals a lot about how the order of visual images shapes who we are, what we know, and how we act.

For example, editing is one of the many ways films hail audiences. The camera angles, the boundaries of each camera shot, and the relationships established between shots position the viewer in relation to the images. Films from the Classical Hollywood era often position the audience as men watching women. In such instances, the camera takes the position of a male character's line of sight as he watches a woman. The viewer is inserted into this point of view. The camera frames the woman in the film as an object that is being viewed. Sometimes the camera frames the woman, or parts of her body, from the view of an omnipotent narrator, who is often the male director. This film structure, called the "male-gaze," endures through contemporary times.

Once a viewer assumes the position from which they are hailed, they become interpellated into a worldview, called ideology. The act of assuming the male-gaze position entails many ideas and ideologies about gender. For instance, men are whole and active; women are passive and often a fragmentation of parts; men look; women are to be looked at. More recently, alternative points of view can be found in popular films and television, especially since we have more minority creators.[1] E. Ann Kaplan (1988) points to the variety of gazes found in the editing of rock videos on music television. She links the continually changing and ambiguous gazes of many rock videos to the identity of the typical MTV viewer. By inserting the viewer into multiple gazes, the music videos "reproduce the decentered human condition that is especially obvious to the young adolescent" (p. 137). Kaplan's critique points out how the editing of images and the psychological experience of the adolescent meet in form.

One can have a better understanding of camera gazes and their implied identities and ideologies through knowledge of editing.[2] Editing, similar to organization, is about putting boundaries around images and establishing relationships among them. The film/video editor, in coordination with the writer and director, organizes shots into scenes and scenes into sequences. These parts assume relationships similar to standard verbal organizational patterns. In the previous chapter, we moved from the more abstract central idea to the more specific subordinate ideas. Here, we begin with the most basic meaningful image visible to the critic's eye, the camera shot, and move through scenes to sequences.

Parts and Principles of Editing

A **shot**, also called a **cut**, is one uninterrupted sequence of action recorded with one camera. A man eating dinner could be captured in one shot. Film and video makers will typically capture one action in several shots, often with more than one camera. For instance, one camera may be positioned in front of the man eating dinner and another camera may be positioned at his right side. Shots of various types and lengths may be taken from each position and then reorganized during the editing process. In such a case, a scene of a man eating dinner would include many shots that could be edited out of their natural sequence. Here, I offer the most basic vocabulary of shots.[3] Shots are of different types, angles, movements, and lengths of time.

Camera Shots and Angles

If you have ever taken a photograph of an object, you have framed a shot. If your camera has only one focal lens, you would physically move closer and further from the object until you frame it in an interesting or appealing manner. You might, for instance, want a picture of a house that includes the yard. Increasing the distance between yourself and the house allows for more of the yard, but the image of the house becomes smaller. Most cameras today have adaptable focal lengths, which allow you to frame the shot in several different ways without changing your distance from the house. Unlike the fixed focal length, adaptable focal lengths maintain the size of the house as the lens pulls back to reveal the surrounding trees.

The ability to change the distance between camera lens and object allows for several types of shots, ranging from the **extreme long shot,** which shoots an object from a great distance, to an **extreme close-up,** which captures the object as it appears very close to the camera lens. Often used to inform viewers of the location of a story, extreme long shots reveal the focus of the shot, or object of the photograph, within its surroundings. An extreme long shot could show a man eating dinner at a counter in the airport, but the shot would also include the many restaurants, ticket counters, departure and arrival gates, and other people going about their business at the airport. The extreme close-up, on the other hand, excludes background and emphasizes the object of the photograph. The extreme close-up might, for instance, show only the man's mouth as he chews his food. The extreme close-up usually offers the audience a distorted view of an object, because people do not and cannot isolate an object in their field of view or view objects from such a close range without cameras and special lenses. In this way, the camera does lie.

More common types of camera shots fall between these two extremes. A **long shot** typically captures the entire body of a person (or several people), if a person is the focus of the shot, and some of the surroundings. Such a shot would capture the man eating his dinner at a counter, as well as the newsstand next to the sandwich shop and people bustling about within the immediate area. A **medium shot** captures the man from the waist up, and less of his immediate surroundings. A **close-up shot** focuses on an object and not its surroundings but would not be as distorting as an extreme close-up. A close-up of the man having dinner would capture his face and maybe his shoulders.

The camera may assume different angles within the shot. Camera angles range from **high angle** to **low angle** shots with an **eye-level angle** positioning the camera parallel to the object of focus. If that object was a person, the camera would be at eye-level. **Point-of-view shots,** which follow the view of the subject(s) on the screen, are sometimes taken at an angle to convey the subject's attitude or perspective.

Returning to the man eating dinner, let us assume he is being shot at eye level in a series of medium shots and close-ups. These shots are followed with a high angle, medium shot of a fork on the floor. The high angle would suggest he is looking at the fork from his position at the counter. A low angle shot would look at the man from the position of the fork, or capture the fork from the position of someone on the floor. The low angle shot is unlikely in this scenario because it would confuse the audience as to the narrator.

Films presenting a realistic view will use the eye level camera to represent an omnipotent narrator, the audience's view point, or one or more characters in the story. If the character is on the ground and looking up, then the low angle shot would be appropriate. A low angle shot would also be appropriate if the story adopted the perspective of a small animal, such as a dog, or an otherwise nonrealist perspective. Finally, point-of-view shots follow the eyes of a character or characters. We have a point-of-view shot if the camera follows the sightline of the diner as he looks across the counter to a couple arguing. The point of view can change, as it would if the next shot captures our diner from the position of the couple.

Camera Movements and Duration

The camera may be motionless or moving. The basic ways a camera moves are by **panning, tilting, craning, dollying, trucking,** and **zooming.** Panning cameras move right and left, whereas tilting cameras move up and down. In pans and tilts the camera may be handheld or positioned on a tripod. Panning and tilting are ways of presenting point-of-view shots and/or following the actual movement of a character or object within a shot, without moving the camera from its position.

In crane, dolly, and truck shots, the entire camera moves. The crane shot is accomplished, as the name implies, by a camera connected to a crane that moves in all directions. Dolly and truck shots place the camera on a dolly or moving vehicle, and move horizontally and vertically, respectively. A crane might be useful shooting firefighters putting out the flames of a burning high-rise building. The crane can move the length and width of the building, as well as into spaces unavailable to a stationary camera lens. A dollying camera could convey more of the movement and action of a runner than a pan shot of the same runner. Unlike all of these movement shots, a zoom shot involves only the lens of the camera; the camera lens, not the camera, moves from far away to a close-up shot. Zoom shots are typically smoother, quicker, and more discreet than other camera movements. Zoom shots are believed to influence audiences in ways that are different from moving cameras:

> There are certain psychological differences between zoom shots and those shots that actually involve a moving camera. Dolly and crane shots tend to give a viewer a sense of entering into or withdrawing from a set: Furniture and people seem to stream by the sides of the screen, as the camera penetrates a three-dimensional space. Zoom lenses tend to foreshorten people and flatten space. The edges of the image simply disappear at all sides; the effect is one of sudden magnification. Instead of feeling as though we are entering a scene, we feel as though a small portion of a scene has been thrust toward us when we view a zoom. (Giannetti, 1982, p. 72)

Also important to the meaning of a shot is its length, that is, the amount of time that a camera shot remains fixed on its object of focus. Most film and television shots are only seconds long but can theoretically last days. In the 1960s, Andy Warhol made a film, appropriately called *Sleep,* from one 8-hour shot of a man sleeping. Warhol only interrupted the shot when he had to change film reels.

When shots of various lengths are combined into a text, they form a rhythm. Music videos are shot with special attention to rhythm, but structural rhythm, or form, is unavoidable in film and video. Viewers can be teased with very brief shots that do not allow them to make sense of the information in the shots, or they can be made uncomfortable with shots that are unusually long. The film *Kids* (1995) created anxiety through a series of seemingly unending close-up shots of sexual activity.

Shots conclude whenever the camera stops. Between shots, the screen image "goes to black," "fades to black," or "dissolves into another shot." **Cuts, fades,** and **dissolves** are comparable to transitions in a speech as they connect ideas for the viewer. For instance, a cut to black typically suggests a greater break in the action than a fade or a dissolve. When film was young and viewers were unaccustomed to visual "grammar," filmmakers would include very explicit transitions, such as written subtitles to inform viewers that it is "later the same day" or a quick shot of a flying plane to inform viewers of the change in location. Today, we barely notice visual transitions in film and video, but they are significant to making meaning.

Boundaries and Relationships

As complex as shots may be, they are but one layer of meaning in film and video. Shots are combined with other shots to form **scenes** and **sequences**. Scenes are determined by location. Any shot or series of shots taken at the same location form a scene. The shots of the airport diner add up to a scene. They may be followed by a scene of teenagers driving around the city looking for a woman. Our film might then return to the airport diner, but this would be considered a third scene. The fourth scene could be a woman getting onto a train.

Viewers relate scenes into sequences by theme, character, action, or time. In our ongoing illustration, all of the airport scenes form a sequence of their own about the diner. The scenes of the teenagers cruising in their car may join with scenes of the woman on the train in a sequence about a teen looking for his mother. At this point, our film has four scenes but two sequences. Sequencing changes as scenes unfold. Imagine we add several scenes to our hypothetical film: Scenes of the diner leaving the airport and making a phone call would change the airport sequence into a sequence about the man; a scene that brings together the diner and the woman on the train would alter the relationship among all the preceding scenes. The constant reformulation of sequences maintains attention and is particularly useful in creating suspense.

The placement of shots within scenes and sequences shapes meaning. A shot of a man running will mean something different if followed by a shot of another man running than if followed by a shot of a train pulling out of a station. Similar to the organization of a speech, the arrangement of shots, scenes, and sequences forms an overall organizational pattern.

For instance, a documentary on the African elephant may be arranged topically by presenting different roles the elephant has played in history or by problems and solutions regarding the extinction of the elephant. A visual text can be comparative through what is called parallel editing.

Parallel editing compares the action at different scenes by alternating shots of the scenes. A filmmaker, for example, would invite the audience to compare sisters through parallel shots of the sisters preparing for a party and an exam, respectively. A narrative structure, quite common in film and video, is a type of chronological structure involving characters in a series of events that rise in tension and then conclude. Narratives include a narrator and a setting that can be suggested quite subtly through the framing and editing of images. One extreme long shot can establish the overall setting of the story. By using only close-up shots, a filmmaker can keep the location of the story a mystery. Point-of-view shots will suggest a narrator.

Regardless of the overall or specific visual structures, audiences tend to expect and value continuity in visual messages, just as they do in spoken and written messages. As an audience, we want to know how the pieces of the communication—in this case, shots, scenes, and sequences—relate to one another. We expect spatial and temporal relationships to be coherent. An editing technique called a **jump cut** violates the continuity principle by disjointing space and time between shots. A point-of-view shot from our diner followed by a shot of stampeding elephants would seemingly "jump" both time and space, unless the elephants are stampeding into the diner.

Jump cuts, once taboo in mainstream film and video, are becoming more acceptable, even popular. Television shows such as *Hill Street Blues, Miami Vice,* and, most recently, *Homicide: Life on the Street* frequently employ jump cuts. Many music videos seem to be constructed entirely of jump cuts. Ultimately, it is the audience that determines the continuity of a visual message. Audiences born since the advent of television, and very familiar with visual grammar (Gumpert & Cathcart, 1985) can tolerate, or perhaps make sense of, seemingly discontinuous images.

In review, images—whether considered through the vocabulary of style, semiology, or metaphor—are structured. To think critically about the structure of images is to examine the editing process as it is experienced by particular audiences. Editing is a terministic screen, directing viewers to perceive images in a particular guise. As with the organization of speeches, critics can examine the introductions and conclusions of film and video. Images always have themes and sometimes a thesis. Also similar to speech organization, the placement of ideas and the amount of space dedicated to ideas affect the meaning of a film or video. The critic interested in editing concentrates on how shots, scenes, and sequences establish boundaries and relationships among ideas. The following questions and answers use the vocabulary of editing to think critically about the structure of a documentary film.[4] As always, the questions must be considered in light of a particular audience and context.

Critical Questions and Answers

The critical comments that follow the questions are taken from Thomas Benson's (1980/1984) critical study of the structure of Fredrick Wiseman's 1968 documentary film, *High School*. Benson uses the vocabulary of editing and organization to think through the structure of the film.

1. Does the editing of the communication text fulfill the creator's purpose? Explain.
Critical comment on effectiveness: Benson concludes the film's structure is clear and persuasive. The introduction and conclusion of the documentary emphasize the film's thesis that schools socialize citizens just as factories produce products:

In the first sequence, a series of traveling shots, Wiseman opens the second shot with a close-up of the back of a milk truck advertising "Penn Made Products," a pun for the Pennsylvania-made products turned out by the school. And when the school first appears, it looks like a factory. The end of the film shows us the product: Students adapted to military service, which seems to stand as a symbol for alienated conformity. (p. 83)

The body of the film relates the themes "power, authority, alienation, sexuality," and "boredom" into a structure that persuades the audience by allowing it "to work its own way through the ambiguous discomforts of the school's oppressiveness and repressiveness. In this way the film becomes an experience before it becomes evidence." (p. 105)

2. Does the editing present the world, ideas about the world, or both, truthfully and ethically?
Critical comment on truth and ethics: Wiseman "leaves his viewers believing that they know the truth about a particular group of human beings . . . but he may be misleading." Wiseman's fragmented images of people's actions and his close-up shots of various body parts are unnec-

essarily manipulative. Wiseman may compromise his humanistic perspective "by his occasional willingness to sacrifice the full humanity of his subjects to make a point" (p. 110). Nevertheless Wiseman rings true to the viewers by recreating "the conflicts of their own adolescent years, and thereby helps them to understand and transcend those conflicts" (p. 110).

3. **How does the editing of the communication text shape identities, ideas, and actions?**
Critical comment on identities, ideas, and actions: The structure of *High School* invites "us to feel angry about the power of the school without quite realizing why" (Benson, p. 89).

In *High School* we have a film that is making a social comment on how institutions produce individuals. If the film is effective in the way Benson suggests, then the audience is likely to feel angry "without quite realizing why." The power of critical thinking is that it helps us to understand why. Benson's critical study suggests the film's editing of images shapes the identity of the people in the film and the people who watch the film. He asks the film's audience to consider the ethics of film shots that suggest limited identities for adolescent high school students (blooming sexuality) and the school's authorities (sexual, powerful, and manipulative). He also asks viewers of *High School* to consider how their own beliefs, attitudes, and experiences participate in the meaning of the film. In other words, the film may be a documentary but it is not documenting an objective world of high schools. When we are conscious of the reasons for our anger, we are in a better position to affect positive social change. When used as a critical tool, the vocabulary of editing reveals reality in the making.

NOTES

1. The male gaze is not easy to overcome, even with women directors. Some would argue that women directors (and women in general) have come to identify with the male gaze.
2. There is controversy over how much control viewers have in the ways they are positioned in film and video. For a good overview of the issues and positions involved in this controversy see Morley, 1989.

3. For a more sophisticated understanding of camera shots in particular, and editing in general, I recommend Butler (1994), Giannetti (1982); Pincus (1972); and Reisz & Millar (1980).

4. A critic can also consider the structure of images through semiological lenses (How are the signs combined with other signs?). Thinking about visual structures through the semiological perspective is especially useful for understanding microstructures, such as the placement of objects and colors within a shot. Thinking about visual structures through the critical questions in this chapter yields more insight into the overall structure of a text.

8 Structure as Narrative

People structure meaning into stories, also called narratives. Narrative structures can be seen from within the framework of classical organization and editing, in which case they are a type of chronological organizational pattern. In this chapter, the concept of narrative is expanded into a perspective on communication that views humans as storytellers and all communication as story (Chatman, 1978; Fisher, 1984, 1985a, 1985b, 1987; MacIntyre, 1984).

Cultures use stories or narratives to shape knowledge and values, maintain social order, and influence action. Many popular cultural narratives teach lessons of conformity: There is no place like home; the good guy always wins; the will of the people in a democracy prevails. In addition to maintaining stability in society, narratives facilitate social change through stories of heroes, their causes, and the villains they battle. Stories provide cultures with memory. The stories narrated by those we call historians are legitimized into historical fact. Narratives are also believed to serve a culture's psyche in the same way dreams are believed to serve an individual's psyche. For instance, the stories of many terror films express and/or assuage our fear of disorder and powerlessness. Stories shape the meaning of human experience. For all these reasons, it is worthwhile to take a critical look at communication as narrative. The vocabulary of narrative differs from editing and organization in a couple of ways. Editing and organization are intentional practices that critics turn into critical tools. Storytelling is also a practice, but the narrative framework to be presented here was developed as a theory for critical thinking. Critics who view structure as narrative find stories implied in art, conversation, and cultural rituals. The vocabulary of narrative, however, is not necessarily inconsistent with the other frameworks for looking at structure. Television is often edited into narrative forms, as are feature films. Speech of all forms may include narratives or, as I will explain, can be critically revealed as narrative.

Parts and Principles of Narratives

Similar to organization, narrative structure entails parts interacting to form a greater whole. Narratives have themes and often they are created for an intentional purpose. A narrative can have a thesis, such as "there is no place like home." The classical parts of a narrative include a **narrator** who describes or implies a **setting, characters, the onset of action,** followed by a **series of events** that **climax in conflict** and then **resolve.**

An easy way to think about narrative structure is to imagine someone telling you a story about an automobile accident. That "someone" is the **narrator.** The story might be presented as follows:

> I was driving down highway 134, just before McDonalds (**setting**) and suddenly this red Chevy pickup (**character**) pulled out from the side of the road (**onset of action**) and cut directly across the highway—all four lanes. I was maybe six cars behind the action, but I saw a big sedan (**character**) smack right into it (**event**) and this caused a chain reaction and cars were spinning out in every direction (**climax**). I pulled over and watched in shock as the police and ambulances (**characters**) showed up to clean up the mess (**resolve**).

The narrative structure can also be used to frame language that we do not typically think of as stories. For instance, a speaker at a college graduation ceremony may present a speech about the challenges of life after college and how to meet those challenges. The speech is clearly structured into a problem and solution organizational pattern, but can also be seen as a narrative. The speaker is the most obvious narrator of the problems and solutions but could be critically understood as imposing another narrator into the story, such as an economist or other expert whose ideas the speaker is drawing on. Taken as the whole, the ideas of the speech may suggest a setting that is off-campus and in the future, that is, "as students go out into the world." The students may be understood as the characters who engage in a sequence of events—in this case, leaving college, encountering obstacles, and finally overcoming obstacles.

Now let us stretch the concept of narrative a bit further by thinking about how a painting, song, or ritual may imply a story. The story of the Jews' exodus from Egypt is explicitly reenacted through the Jewish Passover dinner ritual. More implicitly, wedding rituals suggest a narrative in which characters act out a sequence of events in a particular setting. The wedding ceremony climaxes during the exchange of vows, and resolves itself in congratulations and well wishes. One can even find narratives within the wedding vows. In such a case, you would be looking at a narrative within a narrative. Nineteenth century American painters contributed to expansion of the West through paintings that suggested stories about a vast place of opportunity. In another example of the flexibility of the narrative concept, you could consider how President Reagan often used narratives within his speeches, or consider Reagan as a character in our cultural narrative about America and its political heroes (Lewis, 1987).

The formal vocabulary of narrative serves as a guideline for the critic of communication who is interested in how people in given contexts make meaning through narratives. Not all narratives contain the classical balance of narrative parts, and many times narrative events are presented out of their chronological sequence. It is precisely the choices that individuals or cultures make in their narrative structures that are critically interesting. The vocabulary offered here is a point from which the critic can begin to find alternative narratives.

A critical consideration of narrative necessarily involves the critical study of style, semiotics, and/or metaphors that go into developing the parts of a narrative into a whole. The critic may begin his or her critical interpretation by considering how a storyteller semiotically develops the heroine, setting, and so on. The vocabulary of editing is essential to understanding the construction of film and television narratives. Critics essentially interested in the structure of communication will explore how the placement of narrative parts—and the amount of space dedicated to the narrative parts—influence meaning.[1] For instance, consider how your story about an incident at work will suggest a different reality from your colleague's stories. How much of that reality is shaped by the narrative's structure? The following critical questions and answers employ the vocabulary of narratives to probe the ways narrative structure can shape reality.

Critical Questions and Answers

The critical questions emerging from the narrative perspective can be tackled in part or in whole. It is not enough to simply identify a narrative. Critical thinkers consider how and why the narrative works in a given situation and with what effects.

1. **Is the narrative effective in fulfilling the creator's purpose? Explain.**

   Critical comment on effectiveness: Tarla Rai Peterson (1991) used the narrative perspective to study the talk of interviews she had with farmers in Idaho and Washington. Though each of the farmers had his or her own story of farming, Peterson was interested in the narrative structure that was common among their stories: The farmers served as the narrators, telling stories about themselves, other American farmers, and the American people. The setting is American farmland; the main action is attempting to provide food for America while struggling against government regulation, natural perils, and the speed and costs of technological developments.

   Peterson argues that the farmers' narratives are not effective in resolving the problems they talk about because their story ignores the contradictions between the values of farming and technological progress. Without confronting these contradictory values farmers cannot reconcile immediate and long-term farming goals.

2. **Does the narrative present the world, ideas about the world, or both, truthfully and ethically? Explain.**

   Critical comment on truth and ethics: The farmers' narrative has an unethical dimension in that it presents farming as an intrinsic and natural good, thereby avoiding issues about depleting natural resources (Peterson, p. 303). The farmers' talk and the ideologies it reinforces "limits farmers to a competitive and instrumental relationship with the land, blocking consideration of other options" [such as interdependence with the land, common to Native American thought] (p. 304).

3. **How does the narrative construct identities, ideas, and actions?**

   Critical comment on identities, ideas, and actions: The farmers present their character—their identity—in a complex and contradictory relationship with the American people. The character of the farmer is rooted in the community and yet distinguished by its independence. The farmer is a heroic caretaker of society but a powerless victim of natural and political assaults.

Critical comment on identities, ideas, and actions: The farmers' stories rely on and reinforce the traditional myths of Jeffersonian agrarianism (the farmer takes care of civilization), the American Frontier (the vastness of land offers an abundance of wealth and opportunity to those who explore and develop its resources), and earth-as-a-machine (the earth has a purpose and is controlled by humans).

In review, the structure of most communication can be critically considered through the vocabulary of organization or through a narrative lens. A film about crime and poverty will present themes, a thesis, main ideas, and perhaps a cause-effect or topical structure, but it may also be framed by a narrator who lays out a setting, characters, conflict, climax, and action. Narratives function as do any organizational patterns. They reflect and influence thought and action. In Peterson's critique, the farmers' stories are their identities and ideologies. Peterson is not concerned with an objective truth but with the ethical implications of the farming narrative to ongoing agricultural issues. There are standards for critically evaluating the reasonableness of stories that will be discussed in a later unit.

As a tool for critical thinking, the narrative is a broad, flexible concept that can be applied to different communication forms. There is something universal and poetic about narratives. The flexibility of the narrative allows it to be critically insightful but also overwhelming. Once you understand the narrative perspective, you are likely to see narratives everywhere. It is important to move beyond simply finding stories in symbolic behavior and ask how and why people construct stories as they do.

Note

1. Again, examining the place and space of narrative parts is similar to a semiological analysis. The difference here is that narrative considers a broader structure. As Kenneth Burke (1966) might say, "form in the large."

9 Structure as Drama

Organization, editing, and narrative are, more or less, linear processes. In each case, ideas are linked from past to present, cause to effect, problem to solution, and/or small to large. It is assumed that communication has a beginning, middle, and end. The linear nature of these concepts can limit our critical vision of structure. The structure of the physical world, thought, and language may participate in meaning in ways that are not accounted for in the classical prescription for being organized. Kenneth Burke (1966, 1969a, 1969b), a significant figure in what has come to be called the "dramatistic perspective," offers what many believe to be an alternative view of how communication structures thought and action. According to dramatists, all communication is dramatic action. In other words, people use all forms of language to create dramas that make up the meaning of their life.

Dramatists assume language structures our experience. The idea that humans are actors and the world is our stage expresses a similar view of the world. It is a view that makes sense when we think about a visit to the doctor's office as a drama. Patient and doctor have certain roles to play, costumes to wear, and dialogue that creates and maintains the reality of "the office visit." Even the doctor's credentials are acquired symbolically, through the dramas that are enacted in medical books, lectures, and all of the sign systems related to medical school and practice. Those who borrow the tools of dramatism vary in their commitment to the assumption that language creates reality. However, dramatistic concepts, such as the **pentad** (Burke, 1969a), are most useful when you are interested in how people construct symbolic and/or social realities.

This next section introduces the pentad as a concept for framing the structure of communication. Similar to the narrative structure, the vocabulary of the pentad was developed for critics. Therefore, unlike the classical approach, the pentad is not a very useful prescription for how to communicate. Similar to the other concepts for thinking about structure, the pentad categorizes ideas and draws relationships among them; but rather than relate ideas in time or space, the pentad captures ideas interacting or transacting. Because the pentad offers a different way of thinking about structure, it can take much practice before it can be used with ease.

Parts and Principles of Dramatic Transactions

The dramatic structure(s) of communication can be critically studied through the pentad. The pentad, not as linear as the other ways of identifying structure, approaches meaning as the ever-changing shape we give to our lives. More than the other approaches to structure, the pentad delves into why humans structure meaning as they do—something Burke calls the motive of communication.

The Pentad

The pentad is a critical tool that frames language, or all symbolic action, as drama. The pentad outlines the five essential parts of human dramas as **agents** who **act** in **scenes** through **agencies** with **purpose**. Another way of phrasing the parts of the pentad is **who? does what? where do they do it? how do they do it?** and **why do they do it?**

The pentad is applied to a speaker's words, a filmmaker's images, a composer's words. The pentad is somewhat ambiguous as dramatic structures unfold within and between many texts. The O.J. Simpson trial illustrates the many dramatic possibilities. For instance, an influential drama that emerged from O.J. Simpson's defense team was as follows:

- The agent is Mark Fuhrman, who represents the Los Angeles Police Department.
- The act is framing O. J. Simpson for murder.

- The scene includes the murder scene and all of the places in which the LAPD created and tampered with evidence.
- The agency is the means of tampering such as planting a bloody glove at the murder scene, planting blood in Mr. Simpson's car, and lying on the witness stand.
- The purpose is racism.

Other dramas may be found within the talk of the defense. For instance:

- The agent is Mark Fuhrman.
- The act is lying on the stand.
- The scene is the court room.
- The agency is by swearing that he never made racist statements.
- The purpose is to protect himself and to strengthen the case against Simpson.

The prosecution presented a different reality:

- The agent is O. J. Simpson.
- The act is murder.
- The scene is in front of Nicole Brown Simpson's condominium.
- The agency is repeated stabbings with a knife.
- The purpose is jealousy and rage.

There were many smaller dramas within the prosecution's case. Together, these dramas support one another:

- The agent is O. J. Simpson.
- The act is wife abuse.
- The scene is the home they shared.
- The agency includes his verbal and physical assaults.
- The purpose is his need to be in control and to have power over others.

- The agent is O. J. Simpson.
- The act is disposing of the murder weapon and other potential evidence.
- The scene is the airport.
- The agency is dumping the evidence in a trash can outside the airport.
- The purpose is to cover his criminal actions.

The pentad is a flexible concept the critic can use to shape and reshape a text into different dramas. There are, however, a couple of mistakes critics commonly make when using the pentad. The first problem, common among newcomers to the pentad, is the tendency to apply the pentad to the communication situation instead of to the drama that is created *by the communication*. The dramas of the O. J. trial are found in communication at the trial and communication about the trial. Applying the pentad to the trial as a drama would be simply another way of capturing the overall rhetorical situation:

- The agents are the prosecution and defense teams.
- The act is arguing for Simpson's guilt or innocence.
- The scene is the courtroom.
- The agency is through speech, arguments, and legal procedures.
- The purpose is for justice to prevail.

Applying the pentad in this "extrinsic" way is not a study of communication per se.

The second error, related to the first, is a tendency for critics to conflate the drama *within* the communication and the drama *of* the situation. The part of the pentad called "purpose" prompts the mixing of dramas. When determining the pentadic parts, it is easy to confuse the speaker's purpose—to have the jury render Simpson innocent—with the agent's purpose *within* the drama. Within the drama of the defense, Fuhrman framed O. J. Simpson because he was racist.

These beginners' difficulties with the pentad are worked out with practice and actually serve as a valuable tool for gaining control of reflective thinking. Philosophical thinking, which has been called thought to the second power, shifts levels from thinking to thinking about thinking. The critical thinker knows at what level he or she thinks.

Once comfortable using the pentad, you should gain a more practical understanding of the idea that people construct reality with communication. People interpellate themselves into ideologies through dramatic transactions. Consider the competing realities generated through the O. J. Simpson trial. In its purer form, the dramatistic perspective is not concerned with which of the dramas is true; the competing dramas are all socially and symbolically real. The dramatistic idea of competing realities equalizes differences among people and so we may at least understand misunderstandings. For instance, in an excellent essay, Barry Brummett (1979) uncovers the differing realities of pro- and anti-gay rights activists through a pentadic study of their essays and speeches. He shows how those who are opposed to gay rights frame homosexuality as act, whereas gay rights supporters see homosexuality as part of the agent. According to the first drama one is not gay unless one engages in same-sex sexual relations. According to the second drama, one could be gay and yet never have sexual relations. In the first case, homosexuality is something you do and, like other behaviors, it is appropriate, even necessary, to have laws prohibiting some actions. In the second case, because homosexuality is your identity, no regulation should be imposed.

Philosophical Motives

The pentad reveals more than a formal look at how people structure reality. The pentad can suggest the underlying *motive* or philosophy that gives rise to the drama. Burke, the writer and critic who made the pentad a popular critical tool, suggests that after identifying the parts of the drama, one should determine the controlling parts of the drama. The controlling parts should reveal the speaker's (and agreeing audience) view of the world or overall philosophy. The method dramatists use to determine the philosophy that drives human action is laborious, yet systematic and often quite revealing. Though I find the method too formulaic for everyday critical thinking, I will review the process as a way of illustrating the depth of meaning people create and/or reveal in their dramas.

The critic locates the controlling part, or parts, of a drama by listing all of the possible pairs of dramatic parts as **ratios**. In this case, the ratio symbol: means "controls," "influences," "determines," or "produces." Any drama contains 20 possible ratios that follow in the pattern of

> agent:act (agent controls the act), agent:scene (agent controls the scene), agent:agency (agent controls the agency), agent:purpose (agent controls the purpose)
>
> act:agent (act produces an agent), act:scene (act influences scene), act:agency (act determines agency), act:purpose (act determines purpose)
>
> scene:agent (scene influences agent), and so on.

Using one of the O. J. Simpson defense dramas, we can uncover the following ratios:

Fuhrman:frames Fuhrman:evidence tampering, Fuhrman:outside of condo, Fuhrman:racism

frame:Fuhrman, frame:evidence tampering, frame:outside of condo, frame:racism

evidence tampering:Fuhrman, evidence tampering:frame, evidence tampering:outside of condo, evidence tampering:racism

outside of condo:Fuhrman, outside of condo:frame, outside of condo:evidence tampering, outside of condo:racism

racism:Fuhrman, racism:frame, racism:evidence tampering, racism:outside of condo.

The next step is to ask which ratio dominates the drama. To qualify as controlling the drama, the ratio must carry force, not frequency. In other words, the speaker for the defense may refer to the murder scene a thousand times, but racism has more power over the other elements in the drama. Of the 20 possibilities, those ratios moving from Fuhrman and racism seem to dominate the dramatic action of the defense. Fuhrman is a major player in this drama because the act, agency, and even the scene come into existence because of Fuhrman. But it is the purpose of this drama—racism—that brings all of the other parts of the drama into play. Racism created the scene of the tampering, outside the condo where the beautiful and white Nicole Brown Simpson lived. Racism was behind the evidence tampering. Racism motivated the framing of O. J. Simpson. Racism is what created Fuhrman. The drama of the defense is a drama of racism. Racism, a social disease, implicates all of us. It is no wonder so many of us preferred alternative dramas.

The pentad's elasticity can reveal the ongoing shapes people give to the drama of life. I found that an interesting and easy way to practice thinking with the pentad is to apply it to my own talk, and the talk of friends and family. I consider how friends dramatize the same event differently, and how the dramas reflect some philosophical differences among us. The following questions should help you integrate dramatism into your critical thoughts. You may ask these questions of conversations, letters, paintings, music, poetry, speech, films, literature, rituals, fashion design, architecture, and perhaps more.

Critical Questions and Answers

As with all of the critical concepts, pentadic questions should be considered within a communication context. In the critical case presented here, Marie Boor Tonn, Valerie Endress, and John Diamond (1993) use the pentad to understand how a community, in the state of Maine, absolved a hunter in the death of Karen Wood. In November of 1988, Wood was mistaken for prey by a hunter and shot to death. The hunter was acquitted of murder. The community played out the drama that acquitted the hunter in the press: its editorials, trial coverage, interviews with family members and friends, hunters and nonhunters, Maine natives and transplants. The critics' study of the newspaper dramas is especially revealing because we do not usually think of news reporting as drama or a construction of reality.

1. Does the dramatic action fulfill the creator's purpose?

Critical comment on effectiveness: The press did not set out to consciously persuade the public of the hunter's innocence, but the press accounts of the Wood drama helped to vindicate the hunter. As the drama is presented, Wood is the agent who recently moved to Maine from another state. Wood's act was getting killed. Her agency, or method of accomplishing the act, was not taking the precautions necessary during Maine's hunting season, such as going into the woods in the first place and not wearing flare orange clothing to protect herself. The scene is the woods beyond her backyard—the woods of the hunters, including the one who shot her, who are natives to Maine. Her purpose ranged from negligence to stupidity. In this particular drama the hunter was more of the victim of Wood's carelessness (Tonn, Endress, & Diamond).

2. Does the drama present the world, ideas about the world, or both, truthfully and ethically?

Critical comment on truth and ethics: Tonn, Endress, and Diamond claim the accidental death of Wood and the absolution of the hunter as the cause of her death is consistent and true to the traditions of Maine. But "given a quite different social backdrop and/or differing social status, Wood may have been the "insider" and [the hunter] the "alien," yielding a different interpretation of the act" (p. 179).

3. How does the dramatic action shape identities, ideas, and actions?

Critical comment on identities, ideas, and actions: The drama of Wood's death suggests a deterministic philosophy in which people (agents) are not responsible for their actions. The philosophy or motive is found in the pentadic ratios that suggest the scene is the controlling element in the drama of Wood's death. Wood was considered the agent of drama, but the scene—the natural woods; the place of the hunted and the hunters that make up the state of Maine—brought the agent and the act into the drama. Without the scene, Wood would not have been killed, for she would not have moved to Maine or walked into the woods. Further, there are laws of the land that Wood did not obey. The drama suggests a philosophy that our lives are determined by the material world (p. 166).

Critical comment on identities, ideas, and actions: The drama of Wood's death also reinforces the ideology that the land belongs to nature (and hunters are part of the natural order of things), regardless of who has legal rights or ownership of the land (p. 174).

As these suggestive critical questions and answers show, the pentad is most useful in pursuing how people structure ideas into ideologies, philosophies, and/or social realities. The pentad may also be useful in determining whether the dramatic structure of communication effectively informs or persuades a given audience. Critics can ask questions about the truth or ethics of dramas, but from within the dramatistic perspective, answers are not found in some sort of objective criteria. According to dramatism, unless we can forgo language, all we can know is dramas. The truth and rightness of dramas can be judged by their social implications and by comparing them to the implications of alternative dramas.

In review, the pentad is a different sort of tool for considering the structure of communication. The pentad frames all language, whether it be signifiers, words, images, actions, or objects, into a drama or several dramas. Unlike narratives and classical organizational schemes, dramas are ongoing, dynamic processes. A notable difference between a drama and a story is the involvement of the audience. When communication is a story, there are storytellers and audiences. When communication is a drama, everyone participates in meaning.

The pentad has its weaknesses. First, its ambiguity often leads critics to overproduce dramas without distinguishing among their different layers and relationships. The result is a snarl of dramas that create confusion, not insight. Pentadic ambiguity, however, can be more of an aid than a hindrance. Martha Solomon (1985/1994), a critic who used the pentad to study the Tuskegee Medical Reports, says the pentad is best used as a heuristic: "I find doing more than one 'pass' with Burke's pentad and considering alternate depictions [of dramas] to be a very fruitful exercise regardless of whether I pursue that method" (p 304).

Second, the structure of the pentad often tempts critics into using it as a formula. The formulaic quality of the pentad can be avoided if one keeps asking: Is the pentad leading me to an understanding that I could have come up with without it? The value of all the concepts discussed in this chapter—organization, editing, narrative, and the dramatic pentad—rests in whether they provide some additional insight into how and why people think and act as they do.

Reference List For Unit III

Aristotle (1954). *Rhetoric*. (W. Rhys Roberts, Trans.). New York: Random House.
Benson, T. (1984). The rhetorical structure of Frederick Wiseman's *High School*. In M. Medhurst & T. Benson (Eds.), *Rhetorical dimensions in media* (pp. 80-111). Dubuque, IA: Kendall/Hunt. (Reprinted from *Communication Monographs, 47*, 1980)
Brummett, B. (1979). A pentadic analysis of ideologies in two gay rights controversies. *Central States Speech Journal, 30*, 250-261.
Burke, K. (1966). *Language and symbolic action: Essays on life, literature, and method*. Berkeley: University of California Press.
Burke, K. (1968). *Counter-statement*. Berkeley: University of California Press.
Burke, K. (1969a). *A grammar of motives*. Berkeley: University of California Press.
Burke, K. (1969b). *A rhetoric of motives*. Berkeley: University of California Press.
Butler, J. (1994). *Television*. Belmont, CA: Wadsworth Publishing.
Chatman, S. (1978). *Story and discourse: Narrative structures in fiction and film*. Ithaca, NY: Cornell University Press.
Fisher, W. R. (1984). Narration as human communication paradigm: The case of public moral argument. *Communication Monographs, 51*, 1-22.
Fisher, W. R. (1985a). The narrative paradigm: An elaboration. *Communication Monographs, 52*, 347-367.
Fisher, W. R. (1985b). The narrative paradigm: In the beginning. *Journal of Communication, 4*, 74-89.
Fisher, W. R. (1987). *Human communication as narration: Toward a philosophy of reason and action*. Columbia: University of South Carolina Press.
Foss, S. K. (1996). Judy Chicago's *The Dinner Party*: Empowering of Women's Voice in Visual Art. In S. K. Foss (Ed.), *Rhetorical criticism: Exploration and*

practice (pp. 204-220). Prospect Heights, IL: Waveland Press. (Reprinted from *Women communicating: Studies of women's talk,* pp. 9-26, by B. Bate & A. Taylor, Eds., 1988, Norwood, NJ: Ablex)

Fulkerson, R. P. (1984). The public letter as a rhetorical form: Structure, logic, and style in King's "Letter from Birmingham Jail." In M. Medhurst & T. Benson (Eds.), *Rhetorical Dimensions in Media,* (pp. 296-313). Dubuque, IA: Kendall/Hunt. (Reprinted from *The Quarterly Journal of Speech, 65,* 1979)

Giannetti, L. D. (1982). *Understanding movies.* Englewood Cliffs, NJ: Prentice Hall.

Gibson, J. J. (1966). *The senses considered as perceptual systems.* Boston: Houghton Mifflin.

Gregg, R. (1984). *Symbolic inducement and knowing.* Columbia: University of South Carolina Press.

Gumpert, G., & Cathcart, R. (1985). Media grammars, generations, and media gaps. *Critical Studies in Mass Communication, 2,* 23-35.

Kaplan, E. A. (1988). Whose imaginary? The televisual apparatus, the female body and textual strategies in select rock videos on MTV. In D. Pribram (Ed.), *Female spectators: Looking at film and television* (pp. 132-156). London: Verso.

Lewis, W. F. (1987). Telling America's story: Narrative form and the Reagan presidency. *Quarterly Journal of Speech, 73,* 280-302.

Lule, J. (1995). The rape of Mike Tyson: Race, the press, and symbolic types. *Critical Studies in Mass Communication, 12,* 176-195.

MacIntyre, A. (1984). *After virtue: A study in moral theory.* Notre Dame, IN: Notre Dame University Press.

Mankiller, W. (1994). Inaugural Address as Principal Chief of the Cherokee Nation [Speech]. In V. L. Defrancisco & M. D. Jensen (Eds.), *Women's voices in our time* (pp. 157-166). Prospect Heights, IL: Waveland Press. (Original Speech presented in 1991)

McGuire, Michael (1984). 'Darkness on the Edge of Town': Bruce Springsteen's Rhetoric of Optimism and Despair. In M. Medhurst & T. Benson (Eds.), *Rhetorical dimensions in media* (pp. 233-250). Dubuque, IA: Kendall/Hunt.

Morley, D. (1989). Changing paradigms in audience studies. In E. Seiter, H. Borchers, G. Kruetzner & E. Warth (Eds.), *Remote control: Television, audience, and cultural power* (pp. 16-41). New York: Routledge.

Peterson, T. R. (1991). Telling the farmers' story: Competing responses to soil conservation rhetoric. *Quarterly Journal of Speech, 77,* 289-308.

Pincus, E. (1972). *Guide to filmmaking.* New York: New American Library.

Reisz, K., & Millar, G. (1980). *The technique of film editing.* New York: Focal Press.

Roosevelt, F.D. (1941). Aid to the democracies. *Vital Speeches, 8,* 1941.

Sheehy, G. (1976). *Passages: Predictable crises of adult life.* New York: Bantam.

Sheehy, G. (1996). *New passages: Mapping your life across time.* New York: Ballantine.

Solomon, M. (1994). The rhetoric of dehumanization: An analysis of medical reports of the Tuskegee Syphilis Project. In W. Nothstine, C. Blair, & G.

Copeland (Eds.), *Critical questions: Invention, creativity, and the criticism of discourse and media* (pp. 301-322). New York: St. Martin's. (Reprinted from *Western Journal of Speech Communication, 49,* 1985)

Tonn, M. B., Endress, V. A., & Diamond, J. N. (1993). Hunting and heritage on trial: A dramatistic debate over tragedy, tradition, and territory. *Quarterly Journal of Speech, 79,* 165-181.

UNIT IV

CRITICAL CONCEPTS THAT
FOCUS ON REASONING

As we have seen, meaningful communication takes form in an audience's interpretation of language and structure. "Reasoning" is another dimension of meaning that involves audience participation, and is therefore a critical tool for unraveling the construction of identities, ideas, and actions. Reasoning in communication entails language and structure but highlights the movement of meaning *from* one idea, *to* an unknown or unrecognized idea, *through* another idea. Galileo, Edison, and Einstein reasoned, as do we all, almost all of the time. Most communication moves *from* one idea *to* another idea *through* reasoning. In everyday conversation, for example, someone points out that "you haven't washed the dishes and, therefore, you are a slob." The reasoning, stated or not, rests in the speaker's belief that people who do not wash their dishes are slobs. Reasoning shapes cultural beliefs, scientific knowledge, religious truths, and moral codes. I do not steal from my employer because stealing is wrong. This moral belief emerged in prior reasoning, dependent on earlier reasoning, and so on.

Most reasoning is only partially conscious or explicit.[1] If you were to trace any particular reasoning process to its starting point(s) you will arrive at what is called a "supposition," that is, an idea that the reasoner assumes to be true. Reasoning, therefore, involves a leap of faith. Because so much of reasoning involves subconscious thought, leaps of faith, and assumptions, it is important to become more aware, and yes, more critical of the ways we reason.

Reasoning is similar to structure when you consider that organizational patterns, narratives, and dramas move from, to, and through ideas. Language likewise reasons from one idea to another, through metaphor or sign relationships. The different view of meaning that is generated by reasoning is that it attempts to account for how people invent, create, discover, and/or justify ideas. Accordingly, almost any use of the concept assumes some difference between true and false, right and wrong, consistent and inconsistent thinking.

Reasoning, more than the other components of meaning, implies that some meanings are more truthful, accurate, or believable than others. Reasoning becomes linked to questions of truth because it encompasses the world of things to be invented, discovered, justified, and known, as well as the process through which people discover, justify, and know truths about how the world is. People and the world come together when people reason from their perceptions of the world, or statements of fact, to general beliefs and/or knowledge about the world. For instance, I experienced snow in New York in December of 1990, 1991, 1992, 1993, 1994, 1995, and 1996. From these worldly experiences I reason that what is true in the past will be true in the future. I conclude that in New York, it snows every December. You would think my reasoning was wrong if I concluded that it never snows in December, or that it will not snow this December.

Some scholars believe there are absolute universal truths that serve as the basis for reasoning, and others subscribe to the idea that cultures establish and maintain their own truths. And there are all of the positions in between that recognize different kinds of truths and claim only some of them are relevant to communication. Regardless of the philosophical position you take on this issue, there should be a model (or models) of reasoning that you are comfortable using. As a concept that has captured the attention of great thinkers across time and space, there are many ways to cast the reasoning process. Here, we consider just a few ways to think critically about reasoning in communication: the classical approach to **rhetorical argument, field-dependent argument,** and **narrative rationality.** These three approaches to reasoning cast reasoning into different forms and offer alternative means for evaluating the truth of meaning.

NOTE

1. There is some question about how much of reasoning takes place in thought without language. Historically, scholars in philosophy and rhetoric have adopted different positions on the issue. For our purposes, the question is interesting but not essential because, regardless of the answer, communication critics only contemplate reasoning that is stated in, or implied by, language.

10 Reasoning as Rhetorical Argument

Reasoning is the process of moving *from* an idea, *to* a claim, *through* a third idea. Argument is reasoning in communication. This definition of argument is quite broad, especially when common use of the term limits it to disagreement. The way in which academics use the concept "argument," and the way I will use it here, does not necessarily entail disagreement. Argument is a process of supporting a claim with reasons. Most, if not all, meaningful communication can be framed as argument.

A critical study of *YM* (Duffy & Gotcher, 1996), a contemporary magazine for preteen girls, frames the photographs of seductive women and accompanying verbal text as argument. Even a glance at many girls and women's magazines reveal their emphasis on the importance of beauty to being a woman. But when you think about the images and words in the magazines as arguments, you become aware of the specific beliefs that shape the ideologies of, and about, women. For example, one article in the magazine is accompanied by an image of a young female model positioned with two men. The young woman is "nestled between the legs of the male sitting on the fence, her back pressed against him. . . . Interestingly he holds a rifle in his right hand, a metaphor whose sexual connotations are so well-known that they need not be discussed here." The female model reveals bikini briefs under low-hanging jeans. Her midriff is exposed by a cropped top. Captions surrounding the article read "pop your top," "wear your pants low," and "bare your bikini bottom" (p. 38). Readers will reason *from* the images and captions *to* the claim that "this ideal teen has been able to attract not one but two desirable young men" *because* she has prepared her body and clothing properly (p. 38).

The arguments in the magazine also ask young women readers to believe that they are objects of desire who are dominated by men and that when they purchase the clothing worn by the models they can be the same as the model. These ideas support the magazine's overall claim that women become successful and powerful by being attractive to men. The many arguments that support the claim add up to an ideology which links beauty, sex, love, popularity, and clothing. The ideology is further supported by other articles and issues of the magazine that present "young women with a world view void of occupational opportunities other than modeling, a world view void of educational opportunities, a world view void of intrinsic motivators, a world view in which success is determined by meeting the needs and expectations of males, and a world view free of consequences for sexual activity" (p.45).

The critical reading of *YM* begins with an interpretation of arguments and then moves to ideologies, identity, and action. The critical interpretation of arguments also guides the critic to judge the effectiveness, truth, and ethics of reasoning. In this chapter, we will review the neo-Aristotelian approach to rhetorical argument, developed in the practical context of teaching people how to construct convincing verbal arguments, and reinvented in the 25 centuries since. This traditional approach to rhetorical argument is but one way to identify and evaluate arguments. It is useful for thinking critically about all arguments, including those presented in nonverbal forms.

Aristotle defined two types of rhetorical argument, **the enthymeme** and **the example.** These concepts have been heavily influenced by their counterparts in more formal patterns of logical reasoning called deduction and induction. Therefore, I will compare rhetorical argument to logical argument. First, I will clarify the process of reasoning common to logical and rhetorical argument.[1]

▓▓▓▓ Reasoning in Argument

The process of moving from evidence to a claim is a meaningful unit called an argument. Arguments move to a **claim** from **evidence** through an **inference.** Any part of the argument may be assumed, so let us begin the vocabulary of argument with **assumptions.**

Assumptions are ideas, whether they are beliefs, values, or attitudes, that are not supported with reasons. We are almost always assuming something. Assumptions may be explicit or implicit. For instance, consider some of the assumptions that were made in the interviews I conducted with soup kitchen patrons for a film documentary about a soup kitchen. One of the more explicit assumptions made by a patron is, "When you think of a soup kitchen, you think of really down-and-out people, dirty people and things like that—and they have some of those here, too." The statement is an assumption because the speaker does not provide any reasons for the claim that people who eat at soup kitchens are down and out, and dirty. Notice that this statement also implies another assumption, that is, some of the people who eat at soup kitchens are not down and out and dirty.

Another illustration of an implicit assumption is found in a soup kitchen patron's statement that he did not believe he had a right to use the soup kitchen because "most people who'd go there had poor parents but I was born middle class." He assumes that social services are for people born into poverty. He may also assume that poverty is reproduced in families. Most often the inferences of arguments are assumed but evidence is also assumed. One of the main reasons to think critically about reasoning is to become aware of our assumptions.

A **claim** or **conclusion** is any idea the speaker believes to be true, wants others to accept as true, or both. Politicians build campaigns around claims. In the course of a conversation you might claim that a friend seems "out of sorts." Oliver Stone's film *Natural Born Killers* claims our society is obsessed with violence. A racist character in the film *Pulp Fiction* asserts that blacks are stupid. Daytime talk shows, singularly and collectively assert that some men beat their wives. The hit medical drama *ER* reinforces the claim that medical workers must learn to detach themselves from their patients. Some advertisements make explicit claims but many are implied. An ongoing clothing campaign implies those who buy Bennetton products are liberal and open to diversity. Norman Rockwell's paintings suggest how small-town America was.

A claim does not entail reasoning unless some sort of evidence is present. **Evidence** serves as proof for a claim and typically falls into one of five types: example, statistics, factual data, testimony, and previously established claims or widely accepted beliefs. It is important to identify evidence, as evidence and claim often imply an inference that should be made explicit and evaluated.

Argument moves from evidence to claim through **inferences.** The inferential process is the actual reasoning or connection that justifies the leap from the evidence, "I have seen three cases," to the claim, "therefore in all cases. . . . " It is often a subconscious process that we critics convert into statements. For instance, moving from evidence that involves one case to a claim that asserts something about all cases assumes that this one case is typical of all cases. Though the specific inferences that people make are endless, logicians have grouped them into two logical patterns: deduction and induction. The enthymeme and the example are considered their counterparts in rhetorical argument.

Logic is the study of reasoning as an abstract and formal process of thought. Some scholars, particularly those who study communication, have developed theories of argument to describe and evaluate everyday reasoning in talk.[2] Aristotle wrote about logic and developed a theory of rhetorical argument.[3] The next two sections explain deductive and inductive logic as a basis for defining the rhetorical approach to argument, enthymemes and examples.

Deductive Inference and
the Rhetorical Enthymeme

Logical deduction, as it has been conceived in the Western world, presents a very formal picture of the reasoning process. By formal, I mean that logical reasoning describes, step by step, how people should think. Deductive arguments are analytical mathematical formulas for thinking correctly. The following puzzle, for instance, engages our thought in a very formal and logical process. Find the profession of each man and the color of his shirt.

> Mr. Baker, Mr. Carpenter, Mr. Hunter, and Mr. Walker were not respectively, a baker, a carpenter, a hunter and a walker by profession. They were in the habit of wearing, again not respectively, a brown, a cerise, a heliotrope and a white shirt. No man's profession was the same as his name and the colour of each man's shirt began with a letter which was different from the initial letter both of his name and of his profession.
>
> Mr. Hunter and the professional walker dined together regularly. The hunter, rather curiously, violently disliked the colour brown and would never wear a brown shirt. Mr. Carpenter was the baker. (Emmet, 1970, p. 7)

The process of solving this puzzle involves a series of deductive arguments. Deduction is formal in the sense that we can change the substance of the puzzle—names, shirt colors, and occupations—and the puzzle remains intact. Thinking about the personalities of the men, or the nature of their occupations, will not help you determine the color of each man's shirt.

As a formal process, deductive inferences are logically valid or invalid. A valid inference is not necessarily truthful but is logically consistent. Logical consistency is tested through a syllogism. A syllogism, the formal structure of a deductive argument, consists of two premises and a claim. Premises are simply statements of fact that serve as reasons for the claim. They are, in effect, evidence for the deductive claim. In the typical illustration of deductive form, the first premise, also called the "major premise," is a general statement about "all" or "most" of something. For instance, the statement "Mothers are people who have children" implicates all or most mothers. The second premise, called "minor premise," makes a statement about a particular cases or cases. "Sheila is a mother" is such a statement. From this syllogism, we should conclude that "Sheila, in particular, has a child." Notice how the syllogism can be written in abstract form.

Mothers are women who have children.

All A are B.

Sheila is a mother.

C is A.

Therefore, Sheila is a woman with children.

Therefore, C is B.

Thinking through, or writing out, syllogisms is necessary to reflecting on their consistency in reasoning. Consistency is not truthfulness. You can only question the truthfulness of deductive reasoning by questioning the truth of the premises. If the form of the argument is valid and the premises are true, then the conclusion must be true. Though we are ultimately concerned with the content of the arguments, if the form is invalid then the content does not logically follow.

All of this discussion about deductive inference may seem removed from your everyday life but you can and do reason deductively. And you do not have to solve the previous puzzle to be critical of deductive reasoning. Critical thinking depends on your having a vocabulary for identifying arguments in practical communication. Let us move deductive reasoning out of logic and into rhetorical argument, where the scholastic form of a "syllogism" takes the practical form of an **enthymeme**. In everyday talk, we do not reason in syllogisms. We argue through enthymemes. An enthymeme is based on a widely accepted belief, rather than on an absolute truth or fact. It is concluded with probability rather than certainty. These differences between enthymeme and syllogism assume a difference between beliefs about the world and true knowledge of the world.

In the practical world of people working, loving, buying, eating, and dying, we reason more from probabilities than from absolute truths or facts. When I took my 14-year-old dog to the veterinarian, I was told she "may" have fatal cancer (minor premise). My decision to put her to sleep (conclusion) rested in the "probability" that old dogs rarely outlive cancer (major premise). The major premise of this argument is a widely accepted belief that I assumed. The doctor never said, "Old dogs rarely outlive cancer." The doctor never told me, "Therefore, your dog will soon die." The major premise of this argument cannot be accepted with certainty, nor can its conclusion. I could not, and cannot, be certain about ending that old, sweet dog's life. That is the nature of enthymemes.

The premises of enthymemes often go unstated, because they are based on widely accepted beliefs. Enthymemes invite the audience to participate in reasoning by supplying the unstated beliefs. You can see why it was important to the veterinarian to have me participate in reasoning about the future of my dog. When enthymemes work, they reflect, reinforce, and create ideas and ideologies. However, when speaker and audience make different assumptions, enthymemes create misunderstanding. Returning to the opening illustration of reasoning, a speaker assumes people who do not keep up with their dirty dishes are slobs. By identifying the dirty dishes and calling his roommate a slob, this speaker expects his roommate to also assume that "People who don't wash their dishes are slobs." But what if the roommate assumes "People who worry about dirty dishes are neurotic"?

Identifying enthymemes is a way to reveal the patterns through which people discover, create, and justify their ideas and ideologies. Enthymemes also offer the critic criteria for evaluating the effectiveness and truthfulness of this movement of meaning. A strong enthymeme adheres to some more formal rules of reasoning while at the same time being well-adapted to a particular audience. We will turn to these standards of evaluation after explaining inductive arguments.

Inductive Inference and
the Rhetorical Example

Unlike deduction, **inductive inference** moves the reasoner into the realm of what was previously unknown. Induction predicts and invents ideas. For this reason inductive arguments are concluded with probability. Similar to enthymemes, we can't be absolutely certain the conclusions we arrive at inductively are true. Another difference is that induction is not formally valid or invalid, although inductive arguments can be expressed in quasi-syllogistic form. The premises of induction include evidence and inference, but even if the premises are true, the conclusion does not follow absolutely.

Inductive inference is modeled on reasoning from a statement about one or more cases to a statement about all or most cases. This typical form of inference is called **generalization,** in that the reasoner generalizes what has been true in the past—or true in cases that are known—to what will be true in the future, or in cases we have not yet seen. Scientific studies almost always generalize from particular case studies to the general population—for example, from 500 observed cases to all cases.

Using inference by generalization as the archetype of inductive reasoning, many students of argument define inductive reasoning as inference that moves from particular cases to all, or most, cases. I do not adopt this "rule of thumb," for it excludes many forms of reasoning common to practical affairs. One such form of induction, of particular interest to Aristotle, was induction by parallel case. In many cases of public talk, Aristotle noted that speakers will reason from one particular case to another particular case. Aristotle called this form of everyday argument reasoning by **example.** Today this form of argument is called **parallel case** (Hauser, 1986, p. 74). Twenty-five hundred years of theories of logic and argument have passed since Aristotle, and a variety of nonformal, nondeductive arguments are today considered inductive.

In review, logic has traditionally provided an ideal form of reasoning in deduction. Deductive reasoning that is formally valid leads to certain conclusions. Rhetorical argument concerns itself with reasoning in contexts in which there can be no certainty and where facts do not speak for themselves but require leaps of faith or belief. Enthymematic and induc-

tive forms of reasoning constitute a basic vocabulary for studying rhetorical argument. As a tool for creating or critiquing arguments, the
vocabulary of the traditional rhetorical approach provides some standards for evaluating the strengths and weaknesses of particular arguments.

Standards for Evaluating Rhetorical Argument

The introduction of this unit stated that critical concepts for reasoning
raise questions about the truthfulness of ideas. After all, it is through
reasoning that we arrive at our beliefs about ourselves and the world.
These are the truths by which we live our lives. We are not certain about
most of them and are often in the position of deciding among contradictory beliefs. The critical process for evaluating arguments helps us to
choose our beliefs about ourselves and the world. Using the concept of
rhetorical argument, a critic begins by identifying the reasoning from-to-
through, exposing the assumptions and inferences necessary to make
sense of the argument. This step is valuable in itself, because it brings
many unquestioned and unstated beliefs into the open. Many critics
move on to consider the probable truth and believability of the argument
by evaluating the evidence and inferences. The standards for evaluating
arguments that are suggested here are intended for thinking about the
probable and practical realm of rhetorical argument.

Evaluating Evidence

Evidence supports a claim; therefore, a claim is as strong as its evidence.
I have introduced five types of evidence: example, statistics, factual data,
testimony, and previously established claims or widely accepted beliefs.
There are some criteria that are used to evaluate all evidence and some
that are particular to the type of evidence. In all cases, the critic must
consider the audience, for it renders the evidence meaningful.

The source of all evidence should be evaluated by asking who gathered
the evidence that a speaker uses to support their claim: Was it acquired
firsthand, or from another source? In any case, does the source(s) of
evidence have a bias that would prejudice the collection, the presentation
of the evidence, or both? Almost everyone has biases in the sense of
having opinions about issues. Generally, we would not dismiss evidence

because the speaker is using the evidence to support a claim, but the evidence should be doubted if the source has something to personally gain from manipulating the evidence. A cereal company's studies on the health benefits of bran may be doubted because of their bias to profit.

The date of the evidence is significant, although what qualifies as being recent enough depends on the topic of discussion. Statistics from 1960 linking highway speed limits to fatal accidents are outdated because automobiles and highways are now different, perhaps safer. Statistics from 1960 suggesting cigarette tobacco causes lung cancer may or may not be outdated. If tobacco, environmental, and biological conditions have remained the same, the statistics may be sound.

In most cases of everyday argument, we do not have access to the source and date of the evidence, which should lessen our confidence in our claims. Begin to note how often someone, including yourself, says "they say" and "they did a study." People present evidence without revealing who did the study, when the study was done, how the study was done, and for what reasons. That is not to say we should not accept claims based on such evidence, but we should accept them with a degree of skepticism. Our skepticism regarding evidence should increase as we consider specific types of evidence and the particular ways they mislead. **Examples** are specific instances, or case studies of a given claim. Robert Dole, Republican presidential candidate in 1996, argues from example to his claim that popular culture ridicules family values. According to Dole (1995), examples of popular culture that ridicule family values through "mindless violence and loveless sex" include the films *Natural Born Killers* and *True Romance* and the music of *Cannibal Corpse*, *Geto Boys* and *2 Live Crew*.

The strength—and some would say truth—of Dole's argument depends, in part, on the evidence. Are these examples accurate? Some people claim the films and musical groups he references are actually arguing against violence. Does Dole provide enough examples to support his implication that "all" or "most" popular culture is corrupt? The answer to this question will rest with his audience. In the speech from which this evidence is taken, Dole was addressing Hollywood producers who would be less convinced with these instances than someone less familiar with the entertainment business. Dole's evidence by example can be further tested by questioning whether the cases are typical and if there are cases that do not support the claim. Hollywood producers might claim that the films Dole mentions are exceptional rather than typical, or that there are many more films that support family values than there are that weaken them.

Examples are often considered a type of factual data, but here we consider them a special type. **Factual data** refers to statements of fact, such as "John F. Kennedy was the youngest man to be elected President of the United States." Factual data, as we have defined it here, is often used as a premise in a formal deductive argument. Other forms of factual data include direct observations such as "the paint is peeling" or numbers that are not manipulated beyond simple addition. "I missed class three times" is considered factual data. "I missed 23% of my classes this semester" is considered a statistic. The significance of distinguishing among types of evidence rests in how they are evaluated. You scrutinize factual data by asking if it's clear, accurate, and specific. Think critically about the factual data that supports the claim that "unemployment has risen this summer." The first fact is a survey, collected through all of the unemployment offices in the country in April, that identifies that 5% of the population is actively seeking work. This is compared to factual data, collected in July, that shows 6% of the population is actively seeking work. The facts may be accurate but are they clear and specific enough to reach a certain conclusion? How comparable are these numbers if you learn that the first survey excluded all of the college and high school students that began looking for work in June? As we will see, statistics involve some additional concerns.

Statistics are more than numbers; they involve the manipulation of numbers. A number, such as, there are 483 people in my hometown, is considered factual data or a statement of fact. A statistic involves studying a number of cases, then generalizing or averaging the sample to all or most cases. It is necessary to reason from statistics because we do not always have access to all cases. For instance, television ratings (the total number of people watching a particular program) are determined by surveying some people and then generalizing the figure to all potential television viewers. A rating of 33% suggests that 33% of all televisions were tuned into a particular program, but only a sample of televisions was considered.

The soundness of this statistic, as all statistics, depends on how the data was collected. Aside from knowing when the statistics were collected and who did the collecting, it is important to know how many people were actually studied—called the sample size—and whether they are representative of all the television viewers they are being generalized to include. For instance, we often hear that 4 out of 5 doctors recommend brand X. Would you find the statistic convincing if you learned that only 5 doctors were sampled? Further, what if the doctors were all given free samples of brand X? Or, how believable is this statistic if the five doctors never had the need to prescribe brand X?

In another case of questionable statistics, consider how your total sales with a company might be statistically averaged to support the claim that you consistently work hard. Imagine you sold nothing all year but were lucky at year's end and sold a big ticket item for $100,000. Your sales would average out to be more than $8,000 a month.

Testimony is a quote from someone who offers an interpretation or opinion. Testimony may or may not be rooted in other evidence, including additional testimony. I might support my claim that capital punishment does not reduce crime with testimony from the once Governor of New York, Mario Cuomo. Unless I know the evidence for Cuomo's claims, my reasoning rests entirely on Cuomo's character.

Biased testimony calls into question the integrity of the evidence. For example, I was recently quoted in my college newspaper as stating that "students who graduate with degrees in speech communication typically find jobs within the field of their choice within one year." Although I believe my statement, I do have a bias that could taint my opinion. After all, if there are not enough students interested in studying speech communication, I am out of a job. And, my department is likely to lose potential students if those who study speech communication do not obtain desirable jobs after graduating. A critical thinker would question the integrity of my testimony in this case. I make a claim about "students who graduate in speech communication." One should question, "What students? How many? What makes them typical students?" I claim, these students "find jobs within the field of their choice within one year." One should ask, "What jobs? How and when did you acquire this information?"

These questions are actually probing the evidence that I base my opinion on. In this case, I did survey all of the graduates from the Department of Speech Communication in my college over the last 10 years. The majority of those responding did find jobs within the field of their choice within one year. My survey could be considered factual data or a statistic. In any case, it is pretty vague. Notice that although I surveyed all of the graduates in the last 10 years, my data is based only on those who responded. A critical thinker will have many more questions than conclusions about this "survey." Most human reasoning draws conclusions within degrees of probability, or with exceptions, doubts, or both. The imperfection of evidence is only one of the potential weaknesses in rhetorical argument. Every component in the reasoning process may be more or less problematic. Let us now consider inferences.

Evaluating Inferences

All inferences, stated or implied, are prone to particular errors in reasoning that will be explained here. I will review some of the more common inferences in Western argument, as well as some of their common problems.

Inference by **classification, categorization,** or **definition** classifies, categorizes, or defines persons, places, and/or things, and draws conclusions about them based on their class membership. I heard such an inference just this morning on my favorite talk-radio program, featuring psychologist Dr. Joy Brown. A caller was concerned that her son's cruelty to animals meant that he would be a serial killer, because she heard "serial killers were abusive to animals when they were children." The following arguments exemplify reasoning by classification. They are enthymemes in that they are not based on absolute truths and they cannot be concluded with certainty. If these arguments were made in real-life situations, one or more of the statements would be unstated and assumed.

> Oliver Stone's movies are great.
>
> *Nixon* is a Stone movie.
>
> *Nixon* is a great movie.
>
> Food prepared by my mother is delicious.
>
> My mother prepared dinner this evening.
>
> This evening's dinner will be delicious.
>
> People who grow up to be serial killers are cruel to animals as children.
>
> The unabomber is a serial killer.
>
> The unabomber was cruel to animals as a child.

It is considered a formal error when the reasoner reverses the terms in the inference. As an illustration, recall the caller's argument on the talk-radio show. In the course of her conversation with the psychologist, the woman asserted that she believed serial killers were, as children, animal abusers. She also identified her child as an animal abuser. The woman concluded that her child will grow up to be a serial killer. Her "illogic," if you will, is that even if it is the case that all serial killers were once animal abusers, all animal abusers do not become serial killers.

A second type of inference is **hypothetical case.** In such a case, one infers a hypothetical situation in the form of "If X happens, then Y will follow." The caller's argument about the serial killer takes the hypothetical form when it is expressed as "If a child abuses animals then he will become a serial killer." Reversal of terms invalidates hypothetical arguments as well. No "If X then Y" statements can be reversed into an "If Y then X statement."

The third form of inference, **disjunction,** moves from a general "either X or Y" rule, to a specific statement about Y, through a specific statement about X.

> Either you obey the law or you go to jail.
>
> You did not obey the law.
>
> Therefore, you go to jail.
>
> Either I take classes this summer or get a job.
>
> I am not enrolled in classes this summer.
>
> Therefore, I must get a job.
>
> You must take Interstate 81, or Highway 11, to get from there to here.
>
> He arrived here from there, but did not take Interstate 81.
>
> Therefore, he must have taken Highway 11.

One of the most common problems in disjunctive arguments is that of a false dichotomy. It is often the case that we present ourselves with only one alternative when there are two or more. For instance, the second argument by disjunction asserts that I either take classes this summer or get a job. Perhaps, I could do both.

Inferences by **generalization** and **parallel case** were discussed as the models for inductive reasoning. Both inferences move from specific cases to a prediction about a future case or cases. In generalization, the reasoner infers that what is true in cases that have been experienced will be true in almost all cases. Children learn through generalization, as did my 1-1/2 year-old niece whose first experience with pumpkins was seeing them come out of my oven. I was preparing them for pumpkin pies and told her not to touch them because they were hot. Later we went to a pumpkin patch where she refused to touch any of the pumpkins because she generalized that all pumpkins are hot. In time, she will learn not to make generalizations without considering whether the cases that she reasons *from* are representative of cases she reasons *to*.

In parallel case, one infers that what is true in one case will be true in another case. For example, there is controversy over allowing a large merchandizing chain to establish itself in my town. When people in town argue about whether we can and should prevent the arrival of the franchise, they argue about this particular store in this particular town. They do not generalize their claims to include all towns or all franchises. One of the arguments that is made is the franchise will take business away from local merchants. Reasoning by parallel case, community members often cite an example of a nearby town where this same franchise ruined the local "mom and pop" economy. Arguments by parallel case are weakened when one can find significant differences between the cases. Additionally, evaluating the evidence—significant in all arguments—is especially relevant to arguments by parallel structure and generalization.

An inference by **authority** is assumed anytime someone uses testimony as evidence. The inference is that we should believe whatever the testimony says. If a famous basketball player says, "Wear Nike shoes," then we conclude that "We should wear Nike shoes." Authority is not a very rigorous form of reasoning and yet it is quite common. I put new brake shoes on my car because the mechanic told me to do so. I stopped eating eggs for breakfast because my physician told me to do so.

Obviously reasoning from authority requires a thorough examination of the so-called authority: his or her qualifications, biases, and reasoning processes. Authorities may simply call on other authorities to support their claim, or turn to some of the other forms of inference. A strong argument by authority will reveal the authority's reasoning. Unfortunately, many of us do not have the time or knowledge to look beyond the authority's claim, into his or her reasoning.

Inference by **sign** states that something points to, or is a sign of, something else. Sign reasoning is really what semiology is all about. Semiology sees all communication as an argument by sign. But as argument, we are concerned with signs as reason giving activity. For instance, in a case of what I take to be very weak reasoning, a colleague of mine said that children who walk before they crawl never learn to read well. I asked if she was making an inference by classification: "All children who walk before they crawl are in the class of people who cannot read well?" Her answer was, "No, I wouldn't say that." Then I asked if there was a causal link between walking early and not reading well. She could not explain how one factor caused the other. Frustrated with my probing, she asserted that she had read about studies in which the majority of early walkers became poor readers. It is just a "sign" she said. To summarize, her argument by sign proceeded from statistical evidence provided by the studies to the claim that early walkers become poor readers through an inference by sign that asserts that walking before crawling is a sign of poor reading skills in the future.

In order to evaluate this argument, we would start with a consideration of the evidence. Although my friend alludes to "studies," I know nothing about them. She, in fact, never provided me with any examples or statistics that supported her claim. Next, let us evaluate the sign relationship asserted, or assumed, in the inference. We need to ask if there are other signs to back the claim—such as that early walkers have poor eyesight—and if there are any exceptions to the association between early walking and poor reading skills.

As I offer this illustration of a weak argument by sign, you may come to believe sign reasoning is not particularly insightful or useful. That is not the case. We trust medical doctors who reason by sign in early diagnosis. Legal cases often depend on signs of guilt and innocence. The everyday reasoning involved in making sense of a film or television program requires many inferences by sign. You might, for instance, decide a particular character's clothing, facial expressions, and/or actions, signify their goodness, insanity, or criminality. You may be right or wrong. Few arguments by sign are infallible.

Another form of inference is **analogy**. In a previous chapter I defined analogy as a stylistic device. As a type of figure of speech, the analogy makes a comparison between two things that are not really similar. In an argument by analogy—or perhaps we should say, in a good argument by analogy—a comparison is being made between two things that are more similar than different. People often analogize marijuana to alcohol, concluding that if alcohol is legal then marijuana should be legal.

The key to a good logical analogy is in the similarity between the two things being compared. Any analogy is weakened by pointing out significant differences between the things being compared. Consider the analogy of a television advertisement campaign. The argument is presented by a woman wearing a mouse costume and eating something that appears to be cheese.

Evidence: "Cheese tastes delicious."

Inference by analogy: "Our product is just like cheese."

Conclusion: "Therefore our product tastes delicious."

This advertisement is unusual in that it explicitly states its inference and is probably required to do so by a regulatory agency. If the advertisement allowed the viewing audience to fill in the inference on its own, it would likely assume the product was cheese, and reason by classification.

Evidence: Cheese tastes delicious.

Inference: This product is cheese.

Conclusion: Therefore it must also taste delicious.

The difference between an inference by classification and an inference by analogy is significant. If the product is cheese and you love all cheese, you will probably love this product. But if the product is only similar to cheese then there is a greater chance of being wrong. The strength of the analogy is found in the product's similarities to, and differences from, cheese. All I know about this product from the advertisement is that it looks like cheese. Food coloring may be the only quality it shares with cheese. Most important, it is not cheese. For me, this difference renders the analogy unacceptable.

Causal reasoning, the last inference we will discuss here, is more involved than the other forms of reasoning as it requires an explanation of how something causes something else. To reason causally is to understand how the causal relationship comes to be. For instance, how do you know that smoking causes cancer? The claim is reasoned through the authority of the Surgeon General and the generalizations of scientific studies. But you do not engage in causal reasoning until you *explain* how it is that smoking brings about cancer.

Ronald Reagan (1981) used causal reasoning to support what he believed to be the economic problems and solutions in America. His economic policies came to be called Reaganomics. The policies were based on causal reasoning, argued in his "Reaganomics" speech.

We know now that inflation results from deficit spending. Government has only two ways of getting money other than raising taxes. It can go into the money market and borrow, competing with its own citizens and driving up interest rates, which it has done, or it can print money, and it's done that. Both methods are inflationary.

Reagan's claim: Deficit spending causes inflation. Reagan's causal explanation: Because the government must borrow money to pay its debts and, in so doing, competes for bank loans with citizens, thereby driving up the interest rates.

In another example from the same speech, Reagan states,

All of you who are working know that even with cost-of-living pay raises, you can't keep up with inflation. In our progressive tax system, as you increase the number of dollars you earn, you find yourself moved up into higher tax brackets, paying a higher tax rate just for trying to hold your own. The result? Your standard of living is going down.

Reagan's claim: Your standard of living actually goes down when you make more money. Reagan's causal explanation: Because you are put in a higher tax bracket, losing more than you gain.

You can see that causal arguments provide more information than other forms of argument. Physicians often diagnose by sign but strive to causally explain health and disease. You may determine the cause of your car problems by the authority of a mechanic, but fixing the car will be hit or miss until you (or your mechanic) can explicate the causal inference. As causal reasoning is more involved than the other forms, so is evaluating causal reasoning. In a strong causal argument, the cause is sufficient to produce the effect; there are no other significant causes for the effect; and the argument includes a clear explanation of how X causes Y. Even if you are not familiar with Reaganomics or economic theory, you can begin to evaluate his rationale according to these standards.

I recently participated in a good example of some bad causal reasoning. I was serving on a college committee that set out to fix the curriculum. The committee reasoned that graduating students have not learned the educational essentials. Evidence took the form of studies that show college graduates lack basic skills and knowledge, testimony from community leaders who work with college graduates, and the committee members' firsthand experiences with students. The committee concluded that the college curriculum was the cause of the problem and set out to change the curriculum. A clear causal explanation of how the current curriculum was failing was never discussed. Though a poor curriculum might be a sufficient cause of educational failure, other causes seem equally likely. Some of the other causes that weaken this argument are the students' inadequate high school preparation, unmotivated or undirected students, and ineffective professors. The committee never considered these causes and went about changing the curriculum.

In review, arguments have three necessary parts, although one or more parts may be assumed. The movement of arguments from evidence to a claim is captured in the inference. The vocabulary of rhetorical argument isolates one claim, evidence, and inference at a time and then chains the arguments into the reasoning process. Arguments are often difficult to reconstruct because people imply so much of the reasoning process and because reasoning involves a tangle of arguments moving from-to-through at the same time. The value of identifying the parts of an argument is to expose their assumptions and to evaluate the strengths and weaknesses of evidence and inferences. The following critical questions and answers illustrate how one critic used rhetorical argument as a guide through the dimension of meaning called reasoning.

Critical Questions and Answers

The National Right to Life organization distributed two antiabortion videos to congressional members, supreme court justices, schools, and broadcasters: *The Silent Scream* (1985) and *Eclipse of Reason* (1987). Here we will consider Robert Branham's (1991) evaluation of the arguments in the films. Keep in mind that these questions can only lead to good critical thinking if you understand the communication context. You must know something about the psychology of the people involved because different people make different assumptions.

1. **Are the arguments effective in fulfilling the creator's purpose? Explain.**
Critical comment on effectiveness: Branham reveals how one chain of arguments in the antiabortion films effectively persuades audiences to accept the claim that abortion is wrong. The films rely heavily on evidence in the form of testimony from doctors, nurses, medical technicians and women who converted from pro-choice to antiabortion. The films strengthen the testimony by presenting the factual data, statistics,

and examples that convinced these experts to change their position on abortion. The films effectively set up the audience to make the hypothetical inference, "If even they [the converts] were persuaded then shouldn't you be" (p. 412).

2. **Do the arguments present the world, ideas about the world, or both, truthfully and ethically? Explain.**

Critical comment on truth and ethics: The antiabortion films *Silent Scream* and *Eclipse* provide misleading examples of abortions, including images of fetuses being evacuated from patients. The examples presented are from third trimester abortions, in which the fetus appears more like a fully developed person. These examples, the films suggest, are representative of all abortions. The film offers statistics of the number of "late abortions" performed in the United States to further support the idea that these are typical abortions. The statistics are ambiguous because "late" abortions range from four to nine months. In truth, "third-trimester abortions are almost non-existent, constituting only 0.01% of all abortions performed" (Branham, p. 416).

3. **How do the arguments shape identities, ideas, and actions?**

Critical comment on identities, ideas, and actions: The critical insights in the preceding illustrations reveal that the films shape ideas from "Abortions are wrong" to "Abortions typically kill fully formed babies."

Branham also uses his study of argument to examine the way the films hail women. All of the examples in *Silent Scream* come from images of women who do not speak. The two women who present testimony in *Eclipse* are nameless, faceless (presented in shadows), and were (one hopes) untypically ignorant of abortion at the time of their abortions. One woman, for instance, does not know how far along in pregnancy she is. Branham, and many others who have seen these films, believe they hail women as "innocent wonders" or "helpless damsels." They suggest that women are not intelligent enough to make decisions about pregnancy and abortion (p. 423).

In concluding this chapter on rhetorical argument, let us review its strengths and weaknesses as a tool for thinking critically about reasoning. Its strength is that it seems quite orderly and precise. The critic of an argument casts reasoning as moving from evidence to conclusion through inferences. Because arguments are rarely presented in complete form, the critic uses the enthymeme as a cast to uncover assumptions. Quite often the assumptions have significant social relevance, and critical thinkers should pursue their implications. The traditional approach also provides some basic standards to apply when critically considering how effective, ethical, and probable arguments are. I believe the films *Silent Scream* and *Eclipse* illustrate the need to ask these questions. These are powerful films. I show them to my students and, to this day, the films change, or weaken, the position of pro-choicers in my classes. My intention is not to influence my students on abortion but to move them to critically evaluate arguments in order to understand how they have been persuaded. My students do not always come up with the same critical comments as Branham but they are often as insightful. And some critiques highlight the strengths in the films' rhetorical arguments. All of the critiques are important when audiences shape their realities according to the films.

The traditional approach to argument also gives us insight into the construction of an audience's realities in the form of identities, ideas, and actions. Though Branham's critical comments focus on ideas and identities, we can imagine the actions that have been effected by the film. If Branham is correct and the film reinforces the belief that women are not smart enough to take a conscious stand on abortion, then women may recede from the controversy. Many people may have been persuaded not to have abortions after seeing one of the films. On the other hand, some people may have been persuaded to never open themselves to an argument from the antiabortion activists because these two films were untruthful and unethical. Regardless, new laws allowing states to restrict abortions followed the years these films were produced. I suspect these films have become part of the supertext that is changing Americans' views on abortion.

On the downside, many find the traditional approach to argument awkward, unnatural, and unhelpful. What seems to be order and accuracy is artificial. Although Aristotle presented rhetorical argument as distinct from logical argument, many scholars cast rhetorical arguments as a type of logic, or compare it to logic. In so doing, they borrow from logic its awkwardness and impracticality. I am perhaps guilty of casting rhetorical argument into an unnatural, quasisyllogistic form: evidence, inference, and claim. And my rendering of rhetorical argument suggests standard criteria for evaluating arguments in all situations, as does logic. Stephen Toulmin, a 20th century philosopher, elaborates on the problems with the formal patterns and standard criteria of logic. His alternative view of logic is the subject of the next chapter.

▦ Notes

1. For a discussion of the history of logic and rhetoric, and the relationship between the two approaches to reasoning, see W. S. Howell, 1956 and 1971.

2. Some of the more influential theories of argument in the field of rhetoric include those of Aristotle, Richard Whately, George Campbell, Stephen Toulmin, Chaim Perelman, and Richard Weaver.

3. Aristotle's theory of logic is expounded in his *Prior Analytics* and *Posterior Analytics*. His discussion of rhetorical argument is found in his *Rhetoric*. Most contemporary rhetoric textbooks frame rhetorical argument in relation to formal logic. Although Aristotle made the comparison, he did not merge logical argument and rhetorical argument as much as we do today. I find the vocabulary of logical deduction and induction is relevant to rhetorical arguments. For instance, the standards of evaluating logical consistency are appropriate to enthymemes.

11 Reasoning as Field-Dependent Argument

Stephen Toulmin, a contemporary philosopher, proposed a "field dependent" approach to argument based on his complaints with traditional logic (1958). Toulmin's overall objection is with formal deductive logic, not rhetorical argument. However, insofar as rhetorical arguments are understood in terms of the logical patterns of reasoning and invite standard means of evaluation, Toulmin's criticisms are relevant. While Toulmin has developed many concepts for thinking about argument (1958/1972; Toulmin, Rieke & Janik, 1984), here we will consider only his model for argument and his notion of field dependence. Before these concepts can be appreciated, we need to understand the problems they are meant to overcome.

Toulmin's overall objection to traditional formal logic is that it does not reflect the way people argue and assess arguments in real life. He reminds us that logic is modeled on formal, deductive syllogisms that are concluded with certainty if the premises are true and the form of the argument valid. In the real world of argument, syllogisms and validity are largely irrelevant. People almost never talk in syllogisms. As a critic, you have to go hunting for the syllogisms that are implied, typically requiring you to reconstruct all of a speaker's words, and sometimes thoughts.

Furthermore, a deductive syllogism does not produce previously unknown information, knowledge, or ideas; the conclusion of a deductive argument is embedded in the premises. Consider the premises of a syllogism outlined in the previous chapter: All mothers have children, and Sheila is a mother. If you are certain about these premises, then the conclusion should not come as any news to you. So it is the case that valid syllogisms are redundant.

The formal standards of validity, according to Toulmin, are extraneous to why most real-life arguments are accepted or rejected.[1] First of all, arguments with premises that are expressed as being probably true, instead of absolutely true, cannot be tested for validity. This prerequisite of certainty eliminates most of the arguments that you will come across in any given day. Second, validity is about consistency, not possibility. Whereas consistency may be important in evaluating an argument, it is quite distinct from assessing the possibility that the conclusion of the argument is true. In real life, one would say that it is possible that it will rain tomorrow because a cluster of clouds moving in this direction is a good sign of rain, not because the argument was presented in valid form. According to Toulmin (1958), considerations of consistency are only relevant prior to considerations of possibility:

> We must surely eliminate inconsistencies and self contradictions before we shall have expressed ourselves in an intelligible manner, and until this is done genuine questions about possibility, impossibility or necessity can hardly arise at all. (p. 170)

Third, validity is quite useless when making everyday decisions about what is probably true. Formally valid arguments are concluded with certainty. Scientific arguments are probable, but scientific probability is mathematically calculated. In everyday experience, probability takes on the very practical linguistic form, "most likely," "probably," and "possibly." No one, according to Toulmin, has provided us with any practical discussion of probability. He takes on the question of how people decide that they can "possibly" win the lottery and "probably" complete the project by the weekend.

Given these problems with the classical theory of logic, Toulmin develops a new approach to argument which attempts to account for the traditional inadequacies. His ideas have had considerable influence in the field of communication because they are compatible with rhetorical argument; that is, less formal arguments based on, and concluded with, probability, not certainty. His ideas have influenced how we teach students to make arguments and critique them. Most relevant to thinking critically about reasoning, Toulmin proposed a structural model for argument that has six parts, as well as field-dependent guidelines for assessing arguments.

██████ Reasoning Through Toulmin's Model of Argument

Toulmin constructs a model for argument by outlining what he says is a field invariant means of asserting and justifying claims. In other words, regardless of what one is arguing about, Toulmin agrees that the structure of argument takes the same form. Similar to logical reasoning, Toulmin's model moves from evidence, also called **data** or **grounds, to** a claim.[2] The difference is that traditional approaches characterize reasoning as moving through deductive or inductive inferences, and Toulmin characterizes reasoning as moving through **warrants, backings, qualifiers,** and **rebuttals.** Unlike the rigidity of the classical syllogism, Toulmin acknowledges that not all the parts of an argument are always present—nor do they have to be for reasoning to arrive at probable claims. A probable claim is simply a claim that is probably, rather than absolutely, true.

In illustrating the model, I will consider all six parts, five of which justify the claim. **Data,** not different from the logical concept of evidence, is the support on which the claim rests. The types of evidence (examples, factual data, statistics, testimony, widely accepted beliefs, and claims proven through previous reasoning) discussed under rhetorical argument are applicable, although Toulmin believes that what constitutes good evidence depends on what you are talking about. For example, consider the legal case of The Cincinnati Arts Center Versus the State of Ohio (1990).[3] The arts center was charged with obscenity for its display of artist Robert Mapplethorpe's controversial photographs. The defense supported its claim that the photographs were not obscene with testimony from art experts who claimed the photographs had artistic merit. The qualifications of experts in the field of art are different from experts in forensic science, and the testimony must be evaluated accordingly. In some situations, or fields of inquiry, evidence in the form of testimony would be inappropriate or irrelevant.

The next component of argument is a rule statement, or **warrant,** which explains how the data leads to the acceptance of the claim. The warrant verifies the step from data to claim. The warrant that connects the art experts' testimony to the claim that the pictures were probably not obscene is as follows:

> Claim: Mapplethorpe's photographic display at the Cincinnati Arts Center is not obscene.
>
> Warrant for claim: The pictures are obscene only if they lack serious literary, artistic, political, or scientific value.
>
> Data: Art experts testify the photos have artistic value.

Toulmin (1958) acknowledges that the distinction between data and warrant can sometimes be confusing and offers some criteria for differentiating them. Often, but not always, evidence or data is stated outright, whereas warrants are implied. The argument could be called an enthymeme if the warrant is a widely accepted belief. Warrants are also different from data in that they are "general, certifying the soundness of all arguments of the appropriate type, and have accordingly to be established in quite a different way from the facts we produce as data" (p. 100). Warrants, Toulmin goes on to explain, are established in a field-dependent manner; that is, the warrant of an argument is found within the field of study to which the claim of the argument pertains.

The warrant, noted above and used in the Mapplethorpe controversy, was established by the Supreme Court in 1973. In fact, the judge instructed the 1991 jury to draw their conclusions from the following warrants, all of which were established legally in the 1973 case: The material is obscene "if: (1) the average person, applying contemporary community standards, would find that the material as a whole appeals to the prurient interest; (2) the material depicts or describes sexual conduct in a patently offensive way; and (3) the material, as a whole, lacks serious literary, artistic, political or scientific value" (Knappman, 1994, p. 788).

In another, lighter example, consider my argument in support of dog obedience classes.

> Claim: Gaining control of your dog through a variety of verbal and nonverbal commands will turn a defiant dog into an obedient dog.
>
> Warrant for claim: Dogs are pack animals and will naturally follow the one who prevails in a struggle for power and leadership; the control commands eventually give the user the power to prevail.
>
> Data by example: My dog Daisy Mae behaved badly until I learned the control commands required to turn her into a well-behaved dog.

In this illustration of Toulmin's model for argument, dog trainers and breeders establish the field of experts who establish warrants or rules of animal behavior. The three remaining components of argument are related to the warrant. The **backing** is data or evidence for the warrant, providing proof for the warrant. The **qualifier** expresses the degree of certainty that the warrant leads to the claim. For instance, "absolutely certain," "fairly sure," and "certain within a.05% possibility of error" are all ways of qualifying a claim. The **rebuttal** notes those circumstances in which the warrant should be ignored, or deemed inappropriate, and the claim exceptional.

> Claim: Gaining control of your dog through a variety of verbal and nonverbal commands will turn a defiant dog into an obedient dog.
>
> Data by example: My dog Daisy Mae behaved badly and then I learned the control commands that have turned her into a well-behaved dog.
>
> Warrant for claim: Dogs are pack animals and will naturally follow the one who prevails in a struggle for power and leadership; the control commands eventually give the user the power to prevail.
>
> Backing for warrant: Lorainne Durchee, dog breeder, and dog trainer for 30 years, has observed many cases of dog owners who won the struggle with their dog by learning the control commands.
>
> Rebuttal for warrant: Unless the dog owner behaves inconsistently.
>
> Qualifier for claim: Most likely.

In review, Toulmin's field-dependent approach to reasoning replaces the syllogism with a model of an argument that may have as many as six parts. Because Toulmin acknowledges that not all arguments are presented in six parts, his model of argument may not be much different from a syllogism.[4] Much more important than his model for argument is his idea that the way we assess reasoning is field dependent. I have presented the model here because the concept of field dependence is best explained through it, particularly the warrant and backing.

Field-Dependent Standards for Evaluating Argument

Field dependence, central to Toulmin's alternative view of argument, encompasses the idea that the way people make decisions about what is probably true "depends" on what they are talking about. Classical logical argument is "field invariant," meaning it applies the same set of rules in the assessment of all arguments (regardless of field). Field-dependent arguments are particular to a field of study, whether it be law, medical science, or religion. Continuing with our dog-training example, the ways that dog trainers justify claims about dog behavior are different from the ways psychologists justify claims about human behavior. Each field develops its own standards for judging the soundness of arguments in that field. Most real-life reasoning, according to Toulmin, is field dependent and should be evaluated accordingly.

Field-dependent factors include a field's particular **procedures** for resolving disputes, the degree of **precision** that is acceptable, the degree of **formality** required, and the **field's goals** (Toulmin, Rieke, & Janik, 1984, chap. 25). Arguments made in a court of law, in a scientific journal, and a televised political debate would, for example, have to meet some very formal specifications that would be different from one another. The field of legal argument values testimonial evidence more than the field of science. Stock market experts will tolerate a greater degree of probability than will war generals.

The most difficult aspect of field dependence is determining the appropriate field of evaluation. Sometimes arguments are established and presented in the context of more than one field, and the appropriate standards for assessing arguments can be contradictory. This was the case with arguments relating to the Exxon oil spill in 1989, south of Valdez, Alaska (Sellnow, 1993). The company issued a public relations campaign to regain its credibility after the cleanup. The public relations campaign argued that the cleanup was conducted according to scientific standards. According to the president of Exxon, his company's response to the spill (data) appropriately met the scientifically established (backing), government approved "Oil Spill Contingency Plan" (warrant). When evaluating Exxon's claims according to field-dependent criteria, Timothy Sellnow shows how scientific research procedures and goals are not always consistent with the procedures and goals of business. For instance, Exxon maintained some important norms of science, such as that the criteria for evaluating the cleanup must be pre-established, information must be openly shared, and one should always scrutinize one's own reasoning. At the same time Exxon violated these scientific norms by adjusting some of the scientific criteria to their particular case, withholding some information from the public, and being dogmatic in their claims. The scientific violations may make good business sense. In such cases the goals of scientific reasoning must be carefully combined with the goals of business reasoning, and Sellnow suggests we develop criteria for assessing this cross-field of argument.

In short, field dependence is less standard and absolute in its approach to evaluating argument, but it burdens the critic with determining the field(s) of argument and coming to know the standards in that field. Toulmin continues to work out his theory of field dependence so it is of practical use. The following critical questions and answers should help you interpret reasoning from a field-dependent approach.

███████ Critical Questions and Answers

The field-dependent approach to reasoning asks that you broaden your analysis of the communication context to include the field of argument. Ideally, you should turn to the literature within a field to fully evaluate an argument. Most of us do not have the time for this sort of full evaluation of ongoing reasoning. Nevertheless, it is best to ask the questions if only to become aware of what it is that you do not know.

1. **Are the arguments effective in fulfilling the creator's purpose? Explain.**

   Critical comment on effectiveness: Josina M. Makau and David Lawrence[5] (1994) critically study the legal arguments in civil liberties cases. They are particularly interested in how the U.S. Court determines warrants for the cases, and how these warrants shape democracy. They identify the increasing use of warrants that allow the government more power over individuals, and the majority more power over minorities. For instance, the Court decided that the U.S. Customs Service did not violate their employees' rights by requiring a drug test because "the government's need to conduct suspicionless searches required by the Customs program outweighs the privacy interests of employees" (quoted in Makau & Lawrence, p. 196). Many claim the purpose of the Supreme Court is to protect the rights of the majority and therefore deem these warrants effective (p 204).

2. **Do the arguments present the world, ideas about the world, or both, truthfully and ethically? (Truth and ethics are determined by the field of argument) Explain.**

Critical comment on truth and ethics: In an increasing number of civil liberties cases, including the drug testing case mentioned above, the justices warrant their assessment by comparing the costs and benefits of a particular judgment. The Court's tendency to apply the rule of costs and benefits to issues of civil liberties rights honestly reflects the Court's function in upholding the rights of the powerful majority. According to this view, the Court never did protect the rights of the powerless, and its new warrant makes this bias explicit (Makau & Lawrence, 1994, p. 204).

3. How do the arguments shape identities, ideas, and actions?

Critical comment on identities, ideas, and actions: By establishing and using the warrant of cost-benefit analysis, the Court has redefined the Fourth Amendment, the right of people against unreasonable search and seizures. Some believe the courts should balance majority and minority interests. Today, the Court serves the majority (Makau & Lawrence). The Court's reasoning may ultimately reflect a change in the kind of democracy we live in.

Makau and Lawrence's critique shows how critical judgments about effectiveness, truthfulness, and effects are often dependent on one another; it also shows the critics' political stance. Their study reveals an ideology of majority rights that is powerful in the United States. Whether a critic is going to view the ideology as effectively serving the purpose of the Court, truthfully revealing the position of the Court, or both, will depend on his or her beliefs about civil liberties in a democracy. Apart from anyone's stance on issues of democratic rights, this field-dependent critique remains insightful. It illustrates how a field of inquiry, in this case legal inquiry, can establish and maintain ideas and ideologies through its reasoning.

Many critics find the field-dependent approach to reasoning easier to grasp than the traditional form and standards of logical argument, and rhetorical argument. There is some controversy over whether Toulmin's model for argument is really any different from the tradition of logical argument: Are the data, warrant, and claim the same as a syllogism? Does the six-part model more accurately reflect everyday arguments? The concept of field dependence has raised some issues as well: Is field dependence just another way of saying that truth is relative? What field do you turn to for standards of reasoning when there are competing fields? For Toulmin, the idea that there are fields of experts and probable knowledge prevents field dependence from becoming absolute or relative. In other words, he believes there is no overriding formula for justifying claims but all claims are not equally true.

One final issue with field dependence is whether you trust a field to produce its own standards of truth and ethics. In a sense field dependence favors the ideas and ideologies of those in power by allowing the existing fields to define good reasoning. Critics are advised to turn to the credible institutions of the day for "legitimate" warrants and standards for making warrants. This problem is one that a good analysis of the discursive formation is intended to avoid. Recall, a discursive formation (discussed in chap. 2) includes the specific rules governing who can create knowledge about what, and how they can do it. The primary reason for a critic to examine a discursive formation is to expose those who are excluded from the process of making knowledge. The concepts of field dependence and discursive formation can work together if the critic holds the field of knowledge itself open to critical inquiry. For instance, Makau and Lawrence reveal the warrants created by the Supreme Court but do not accept these warrants outright. Instead, they consider how the warrants would be accepted and/or rejected by people with different political ideologies. In effect, Makau and Lawrence fulfill the goal of critical thinking that I am emphasizing in this book. They make cultural ideologies and their production more obvious to us, so we have the opportunity to change the direction of American democracy if we choose to do so.

Notes

1. I have not discussed the formal standards of validity in any detail. However, some of the standards for evaluating rhetorical argument, presented in the previous chapter (inference by classification and hypothetical case) include rules of validity.

2. Toulmin refers to evidence as "data" or "grounds," and conclusions as "claims."

3. For a brief description and bibliography of the Mapplethorpe Obscenity Trial, see Knappman, 1994.

4. Indeed, basic speech and writing texts that include a discussion of Toulmin's approach to argument emphasize his model as a syllogism with three extra parts. Often textbooks will even distinguish between deductive and inductive arguments on the model, a distinction that Toulmin intended to eliminate. It is my opinion

that many people in the field of communication have come to understand Toulmin's approach through the framework of traditional logical argument, thereby missing much of the value of Toulmin's ideas.

5. Makau and Lawrence do not present the arguments according to Toulmin's model of argument, but their critical interpretations do assume the language of warrants and field dependence. I have taken the liberty of fashioning the authors' presentation of arguments according to Toulmin's model.

12 Reasoning as Narrative

Whereas rhetorical argument captures reasoning as based on the beliefs of particular audiences and field-dependent argument explores reasoning as particular to fields of experts, those who identify reasoning as narrative see it as an ongoing cultural process in which people invent, create, and justify ideas through stories. Unlike most approaches to reasoning, narrative reasoning is not formalized into the inferential structure of enthymemes—or even Toulmin's model of argument. Stories, however, do have a structure and a method for evaluating whether the story is truthful, believable, or both. A previous chapter described the prototypical narrative in Western cultures as including a narrator, setting, characters, and some sort of a conflict that rises in action and then resolves itself. There are variations of this structure, however, all narratives have themes and often they are created for a specific purpose. This chapter is dedicated to illustrating how these same stories—any stories—can be viewed as reasoning.

Similar to all reasoning, narratives move *from-to-through* ideas; they offer reasons in support of a claim. For example, one critic (Jasinski, 1993) shows how the film narrative *The Big Chill* (1983) makes an argument that strong communities are built on friendship. The film makes the argument through a story about a group of friends who reunite for a funeral and find that they have lost their sense of community. The film reveals different relationships among some of the friends as alternatives for coping with the loss of community. For instance, two of the characters form a bond of intimacy, called "eros." Three of the characters form a bond of friendship, called "philia." One character opts to estrange himself from the community. The film's editing "establishes and then compares and contrasts the norms . . . of the constructed communities." so "the process of narrative argument culminates in the affirmation of the norms of philia" (Jasinski, 1993, p. 468). A critic can also find stories that argue claims implied in paintings or photographs. Biblical stories create and justify moral principles. Through their everyday tales people reason through their identities, ideas, and actions.

Critics who favor the narrative approach to reasoning point to three key advantages that distinguish it from the other forms of reasoning discussed here. First, many believe that narratives are more typical of how people invent and justify ideas. Second, the narrative approach is more inclusive in that it describes how people do reason rather than prescribes how people should reason. According to this position, the neo-Aristotelian and the field-dependent approaches are elitist in that they limit reasoning to those people who have knowledge of the issues, modes of arguments, formal tests of evidence and validity, and people who have the time to reflect on such matters (Fisher, 1984). That is not to say that some stories are not better, or more truthful, than others. In fact, "narrative rationality," the third contribution of the narrative framework, directs the critic to evaluate reasoning from within the world of telling and hearing stories. Before a critic turns to these standards for evaluating narrative rationality, he or she should analyze and interpret the narrative structure.

Reasoning Through Narrative

Recall from the previous unit that narratives appear in different forms and sizes: from campfire songs to federal constitutions, from the grand narratives that emerge in political campaigns, to the personal narrative of a woman talking about her experiences in an American concentration camp for Japanese Americans. In any case, the critic should identify the parts of the narrative structure and the relationships among those parts: narrator, setting, characters, the onset of action, a series of related events, a climax, and resolution.

As a quick illustration, let us take the more obvious narrative form of a movie. The popular film *Independence Day* (1996) presents a story about the United States struggling for survival against a hostile invasion from another planet. The main characters include the president of the United States, his wife and daughter, the president's assistant and her ex-husband and his father, a young cadet, his girlfriend and her son. The main action begins when aliens invade the earth with the intention of destroying human life. A series of violent invasions from the aliens and U.S. military response make up the main events. There are, of course, a series of subplots dealing with familial and romantic relationships. The climax of the film occurs when the earth (the United States seems to be in charge of its survival) confronts its final opportunity to obliterate the aliens. All ends well.

The critical thinker identifies the parts of the narrative and then moves into the interpretive phase of critical thinking by considering the relationships among the parts of the narrative, its themes, thesis, purpose, emphasis, explicit and implicit ideas and ideologies. A full-blown interpretation of the film would take considerable time and space. Briefly, the themes of *Independence Day* emphasize patriotism, teamwork, science, and technology. Some ideas embedded in the narrative are that the United States is the global caretaker; it is important that we are technologically ready for military and space invasions; and research into space is very significant.

So far, thinking critically about narrative reasoning is not different from thinking critically about narrative structure. At this point in narrative criticism the critic can evaluate the narrative as structure, or pursue questions about the narrative as reasoning.

Standards for Evaluating Narrative Rationality

It is not until you move through these more analytic and interpretive questions that you are ready to evaluate narrative(s) as a process of reasoning. Walter Fisher's (1984, 1985a, 1985b, 1987) criteria for assessing narrative reasoning will be our emphasis here, although they can be used in combination with the standards for evaluating rhetorical and field-dependent argument as well. The thrust of narrative rationality, however, assumes that in everyday affairs, people accept or reject stories according to whether they are consistent with other stories they believe to be true and whether they endorse beliefs and actions that they believe to be morally right. We call these standards for evaluating narrative reasoning **narrative probability** and **narrative fidelity**. They are created by the storytelling community or culture in a supertext of cultural narratives. The standards for evaluating rhetorical and field-dependent argument are thought to be separate from, and determined before, a particular argument. The standards for evaluating narrative rationality are determined in a context of other narratives.

Narrative Probability

The test of narrative probability is more of a formal than a substantive concept, asking the critic to consider the internal consistency of the narrative and whether the narrative is consistent with other social narratives (Fisher 1987, p. 47). *Independence Day* had many internal inconsistencies. To mention just a couple of them, the space aliens were not physically similar to humans, but their spaceships were well-suited for our American heroes, who were able to fit into the alien's vehicles quite comfortably and drive them. The cadet and his girl friend not only survive when almost everyone else in their proximity is killed but they manage to find each other under impossible circumstances. Whereas the film's internal consistency is weak, the space alien invasion depicted in the film is consistent with contemporary social narratives about the unabomber, suicide bombings, and other acts of terrorism that occupied public attention in 1996. Thus, the essential structure of the narrative is believable.

Narrative Fidelity

The test of narrative fidelity is more problematic as it touches on issues of truth and morality. The critic considers if the values of the narrative correspond to social knowledge and whether the implications of the values are socially desirable (Fisher, 1984, p. 16). Unlike the universal standards of logical arguments, the standards of narrative fidelity are determined within the culture of the narrative.

For instance, the beliefs and values of *Independence Day*, a popular cultural narrative, correspond to social thought and action in the United States. The film advocates military readiness, ethnocentrism, and personal sacrifice for public good. It also values marriage, family life, teamwork, and loyalty. In my critical judgment, *Independence Day* promotes the allocation of time and money to military science and technology and, of course, space exploration. It may also reinforce attitudes, beliefs, and values that foster anti-immigration policies by focusing on the evil "others" who will destroy us. I ask you the ultimate question of fidelity: Are these values and actions faithful to our cultural ideals?

The standards of narrative rationality, similar to the other ways of casting reasoning, invite mixed critical reviews. For instance, I would give the thumbs-up to some aspects of *Independence Day's* invention and justification of ideas, but other aspects of the film's reasoning were deplorable. There are few absolutes that we know and reason about, so the best a critical thinker can do is identify the strengths and weaknesses of reasoning.

In summary, narrative rationality views stories as reasoning, and arguments as stories. Narrative reframes the structure of argument from evidence to claim through inference, as reasoning from stories, through stories, to stories. The standards for evaluating narrative rationality require the critic to know something about the cultural history of the audience. Narratives are judged according to other narratives. Once again, we will review with a summary of a critical study of narrative reasoning.

▨ Critical Questions and Answers

Assessing the communication situation is important to thinking critically about narratives as reasoning. You should pay special attention to other narratives circulating at the time. You cannot understand, for instance, how the American public reasons with *Independence Day* in the summer of 1996 unless you consider the onslaught of narratives about terrorism and illegal immigration that have commanded its attention. Assuming that you consider the communication context, the following questions and illustrative answers should help you through the process of evaluating reasoning as narrative. In an effort to move beyond the more obvious narratives that are found in films, I offer an example from conversations I had with patrons of a soup kitchen about their lives and their economic poverty (Cohen, 1997). The conversations took the form of interviews that were videotaped for a documentary about soup kitchens. As the documentary was being put together, my critical instincts tuned into the structural similarity among the soup kitchen patrons' stories.

The patrons served as narrators for their own stories and they all chose to talk about themselves, their families, and some of the other people who eat at soup kitchens (characters). The settings emphasized were their childhood homes, the soup kitchen, and a variety of social service agencies in the United States. During the course of each interview, each patron related the series of events that eventually led to their economic poverty.

The soup kitchen patrons emphasized character in their talk. They all spoke about the "good" families they grew up in, families that worked hard, ate well, and refused handouts from other people or social service agencies. They all distinguished their own character from "others" you find at soup kitchens, who are "from bad families," "alcoholics and drug addicts," "dirty and down and out." None of the stories had a resolution as we think of resolutions. Most of the patrons saw their economic poverty as a temporary condition for which they were personally responsible. The resolution, insofar as they suggested one, was their hope for an improved economic future. This is the common structure of the narratives as told by the patrons.

Now, guided by the more interpretive and evaluative vocabulary, I consider the narrative in terms of its effectiveness, narrative rationality, and influence on what people commonly refer to as "reality."

1. **Does the narrative effectively fulfill the purpose of its creators? Explain.**

   Critical comment on effectiveness: By presenting themselves as being from good families, the soup kitchen patrons effectively restore their own sense of integrity that cultural definitions of poverty seem to deny. By contrasting themselves to the stereotypical poor who are from bad families, they attempt to align themselves with their audience's stereotypes of the poor (the interviewer and anyone who will view the videotaped documentary about a soup kitchen) (Cohen, 1997).

2. **Does the narrative present the world, ideas about the world, or both, truthfully and ethically (truth takes the shape of narrative rationality)? Explain.**

Critical comment on truthfulness and ethics: The patrons' presenta-
tions of themselves are internally consistent, insofar as it is commonly
believed that people who are from good families will value hard work
and take individual responsibility for their lives. In addition, the events
presented do not pose any inconsistencies with the characters. In fact, all
of the narrators offer accounts of why they are not working or making
enough money to support themselves, and such accounts of work are
expected in American society.

The soup kitchen narratives are consistent with our institutional
constructions of poverty that have historically divided the good and
deserving poor from poor people who are essentially bad and undeserving. Beginning in the 1960s, well-meaning sociologists, anthropologists,
and policy makers developed the "culture of poverty" thesis that identifies "the poor" by a pattern of attitudes, values, and behaviors that are
at odds with mainstream morality. According to this thesis, poor people
are reproduced by families who do not value hard work or plan for the
future. Although the soup kitchen patrons exclude themselves from such
families, they reinforce the culture of poverty narrative by contrasting
themselves and their poverty to the stereotypical poor. In short, the soup
kitchen patrons' stories make sense in themselves and within the broader
realm of narratives our society constructs about poverty.

The stories do not serve the patrons' or society's best interests. The
patrons value significant themes, such as traditional family roles, hard
work, personal responsibility, and personal integrity, and then use these
values to distinguish between poor people who deserve help and poor
people who do not deserve help. These value themes are esteemed at the
expense of equality, human compassion, physical health, and nutrition.

3. How does the narrative shape identities, ideas, and actions?

Critical comment on identities, ideas, and actions: If we follow the
reasoning in these stories, programs for the poor will be directed at
individual families, ignoring the unmarried, the single, and those who had
all of the advantages of a "good family" but are impoverished anyway.
Also, to presume the family structure accounts for poverty ignores a
complex of related, and possibly independent, factors such as mental
illness, violence, crime, drug and alcohol abuse, and prejudice. Actually,
the distinction between poor people from good families and those born
into poverty through a bad family does not even attempt to help the
latter. These characters are the undeserving, unapproachable, incurable

poor. In short, the patrons' stories, and our ongoing historical narrative rationality about the poor, are not faithful to the American ideal of equality.

My main intention in publishing my critical work on the talk of soup kitchen patrons was to show how people construct identities in talk. This case, in particular, shows how we often construct identities that are detrimental to ourselves. More than that, I think the study of narrative rationality shows how cultures justify ideas and ideologies in casual ways that have significant implications to social action. Our cultural ideas about poverty influence whether those who are impoverished and in need of help will identify themselves as such. Our ideas about poverty will also affect the ways we develop programs and policies to help poor people.

The narrative approach shows promise as a "meta" approach to reasoning that can include the reasoning of different cultures, fields of study, topics, and forms of communication. You may also use the narrative approach with alternative approaches to rationality. The critic can position rhetorical arguments, field-dependent arguments, or both, as narratives or parts of narratives.

The narrative approach has generated some issues among scholars, primarily around the concept of narrative rationality.[1] Is it useful? Is it as formulaic as more traditional approaches to reasoning? I suggest, as with all of the critical vocabulary, that the value of narrative rationality will depend on the critic, his or her assumptions about the nature of meaning and reality, and the object of critical attention.

▓ Note

1. See, for instance, Lucaites and Condit, 1985; McGee and Nelson, 1985; and Warnick, 1987.

▓ Reference List For Unit IV

Aristotle. (1954). *Rhetoric*. (W. Rhys Roberts, Trans.). New York: Random House.
Aristotle. Prior analytics. In J. A. Smith & W. D. Ross (Eds.), *The works of Aristotle*. Oxford, England: Clarendon Press (1910-1952).
Aristotle. Posterior analytics. In J.A. Smith & W.D. Ross (Eds.), *The works of Aristotle*. Oxford, England: Clarendon Press (1910-1952).

Branham, R. J. (1991). The role of the convert in "Eclipse of Reason" and "The Silent Scream." *The Quarterly Journal of Speech, 4,* 407-426.

Campbell, G. (1963). *The philosophy of rhetoric.* (Lloyd F. Bitzer, Ed.). Carbondale: Southern Illinois University Press.

Cohen, J. R. (1997). Poverty: Talk, identity, and action. *Qualitative Inquiry, 3,* 71-92.

Dole, R. (1995, May 31). Untitled remarks by Republican Senator Bob Dole in Los Angeles, California. Text was distributed by Dole for President in New Hampshire and received by NH-Primary@unh.edu.

Duffy, M., & Gotcher, M. J. (1996). Critical advice on how to get the guy: The rhetorical vision of power and seduction in the teen magazine *YM. Journal of Communication Inquiry, 20,* 32-48.

Emmet, E. R. (1970). *101 brain puzzlers.* New York: Harper & Row.

Fisher, W. R. (1984). Narration as human communication paradigm: The case of public moral argument. *Communication Monographs, 51,* 1-22.

Fisher, W. R. (1985a). The narrative paradigm: An elaboration. *Communication Monographs, 52,* 347-367.

Fisher, W. R. (1985b). The narrative paradigm: In the beginning. *Journal of Communication, 35,* 74-89.

Fisher, W. R. (1987). *Human communication as narration: Toward a philosophy of reason and action.* Columbia: University of South Carolina Press.

Hauser, G. A. (1986). *Introduction to rhetorical theory.* Chicago, IL: Waveland Press.

Howell, W. S. (1956). *Logic and rhetoric in England, 1500-1700.* New York: Russell & Russell.

Howell, W. S. (1971). *18th century British logic and rhetoric.* Princeton, NJ: Princeton University Press.

Jasinski, J. (1993). (Re)constituting community through narrative argument: Eros and philia in *The Big Chill. Quarterly Journal of Speech, 79,* 467-486.

Knappman, E. W. (1994). *Great American trials: From Salem witchcraft to Rodney King.* Detroit, MI: Visible Ink Press.

Lucaites, J. L. & Condit, M. C. (1985). Reconstructing narrative theory: A functional perspective. *Journal of Communication, 35,* 90-108.

Makau, J. M., & Lawrence, D. (1994). Administrative judicial rhetoric: The Supreme Court's new thesis of political morality. *Argumentation and Advocacy, 30,* 191-205.

McGee, M. C. & Nelson, J. S. (1985). Narrative reason in public argument. *Journal of Communication, 35,* 139-155.

Perelman, C. (1979). *The new rhetoric and the humanities.* Dordrecht, Holland: D. Reidel Publishing.

Reagan, R. (1981, February 5). *Reaganomics.* Televised presidential address presented to the nation from Washington D.C.

Sellnow, T. L. (1993). Scientific argument in organizational crises communication: The case of Exxon. *Argumentation and Advocacy, 30,* 28-42.

Solomon M. (1994). The rhetoric of dehumanization: An analysis of medical reports of the Tuskegee Syphilis Project. In W. Nothstine, C. Blair & G.

Copeland (Eds.), *Critical questions: Invention, creativity, and the criticism of discourse and media* (pp. 301-322). New York: St. Martin's. (Reprinted from *Western Journal of Speech Communication, 49,* 1985)

Toulmin, S. (1958). *The uses of argument.* Cambridge, UK: Cambridge University Press.

Toulmin, S. (1972). *Human Understanding.* Princeton, NJ: Princeton University Press.

Toulmin, S., Rieke, R., & Janik, A. (1984). *An introduction to reasoning.* New York: Macmillan.

Warnick, B. (1987). The narrative paradigm: Another story. *Quarterly Journal of Speech, 73,* 172-182.

Weaver, R. (1970). *Language is sermonic: Richard M. Weaver on the nature of rhetoric.* R. L. Johannesen, R. Strickland & R. T. Eubanks (Eds.). Baton Rouge: Louisiana State University Press.

Whately, R. (1963). *Elements of rhetoric.* D. Ehninger (Ed.). Carbondale: Southern Illinois University Press.

UNIT V

CRITICAL CONCEPTS THAT
FOCUS ON CHARACTER

Character has reference to the person or persons shaped in and by communication: the musician, speaker, filmmaker, teacher, television producer, artist, and their audiences. This unit considers a range of concepts for critically viewing the character of meaning, from character as the speaker's personality to character as the place in which symbols, ideas, and people become one. Character is an ever-present component of meaning because people are essential to meaning. Consider the character of the communication texts we have considered in other chapters. My critical reflections on the talk of the soup kitchen patrons were essentially guided by the narrative approach to reasoning. Within the patrons' narrative rationality, however, I found their development of character to have significant implications to our social identities, ideologies, and policies (1997). Much of the persuasiveness of the Tuskegee Reports on the studies of untreated syphilis relied on the public's perceptions of the objective and progressive character of scientists (Solomon, 1985/1994). Newspaper coverage of the shooting death of Karen Wood identifies the character of the hunter as natives who have a history with, and right to, nature; their character represents the cultural heritage of Maine (Tonn, Endress, and Diamond, 1993).

A critic locates character in an audience's perceptions and conceptions of the speaker, his or her language, structure, and reasoning. A speaker does not reveal his or her character as much as an audience constructs that character. As is always the case with meaning, the audience's assumptions are important. The character of Minister Louis Farrakhan depends on how his audiences think about race, religion, and politics. We know, if we have followed media coverage of Farrakhan, that he has at least two characters: He is racist and anti Semitic to some, and a great, moral, Muslim leader to others. An audience's participation in meaning also implicates its own character. In other words, your own character is shaped by the audiences you are willing to be.

The difference between character and the other dimensions of meaning is, once again, a matter of focus. Sometimes one dimension of meaning stands out as particularly relevant. For instance, Jesse Jackson's use of language seems particularly influential. His character is controversial and therefore also quite relevant to the meaning of his talk. Sometimes a critic is curious about a particular dimension and chooses to bring it into focus for a variety of reasons. I may, for instance, decide to examine Jesse Jackson's arguments because they seem to get lost in the passion of his style. In any case, the critical concepts afford the critic a particular view of communication.

All of the concepts for character, to be discussed in this unit, can be used in combination with the critical vocabulary presented in previous chapters. **Ethos** is the classical lens for framing the role of a speaker's character in meaning. **The second persona** is a concept that is especially useful for considering the character of an audience or culture that is implied in meaning. **Identification,** the final character-specific concept to be discussed here, is a bonding of sorts, where symbols and people become one. Regardless of the sense of the concept a critic finds most useful, character is directly related to the identity of all who participate in communication.

13 Character as Ethos

Aristotle asserted the importance of a speaker's character in effectively persuading an audience. His words remain relevant today. Consider how the following statement Aristotle made in the *Rhetoric* applies to the trial of the Menendez brothers, the oratory of Reverend Jesse Jackson, or even the promotions for Banana Republic Clothing Stores: "The orator must not only try to make the argument of his speech demonstrative and worthy of belief; he must also make his own character look right" (p. 90).

Making one's self believable remains important to speakers and, nowadays, their public relations teams. The character that is implied or shaped by communication is always more or less of a factor in meaning.

Ethos, or ethical proof, has come to be thought of as an Aristotelian concept but has really evolved through interpretations and extensions of Aristotle's *Rhetoric*.[1] Aristotle claimed speakers make their words believable by convincing the audience of their **good sense, good moral character,** and **good will.** Though variations of these qualities have been explored over the years, most of them can be accounted for within Aristotle's qualities of ethos. Similar to the neo-Aristotelian qualities of effective style, the critic will find it most useful to explore how the qualities of ethos function in a particular communication context.

The Qualities of Ethos

Believable speakers demonstrate **good sense**. Good sense is narrowly defined as intelligence in the form of knowledge and reasoning skills. A speaker could, however, demonstrate good sense through all of the components of meaning. For instance, we could say that, generally, an articulate speaker will be perceived as having good sense because he or she uses language clearly and vividly. A musician may demonstrate intelligence through musical innovations and skills. In any case, signifiers of good sense are only partially provided by the speaker, because the audience will ultimately judge whether the language is clear and the musical arrangement is innovative. The audience's preconceived beliefs about the speaker will influence its perception of his ethos. If the audience believes a speaker is simple minded, it is unlikely to be favorably impressed by his evidence. The believable speaker will build a stronger case by bringing in good moral character and good will as further proof of ethos.

   Strong moral character is created by associating oneself with virtuous goals. One strategy for doing so, a strategy most of us have used at sometime in our life, is to raise oneself by condemning someone else. This strategy is often used as a defense strategy for those accused of violent crimes. Though such a strategy may be effective in the short term, we have seen that repeated instances of putting others down typically hurts an audience's perception of a speaker's moral character. President Richard Nixon serves as a good example. In the 1950s, at the beginning of his political career, Nixon often attacked others and blamed them for his failures (the Democrats, the communists). Such attacks worked to his advantage for a short while. After many years of speaking in public and continuing his attacks on others (Democrats, communists, the press, the vocal minority), Nixon was perceived as paranoid and accusatory. Boosting one's own moral character by maligning others is a strategy that is inconsistent with the qualities people tend to bestow on the virtuous.

   Aristotle describes the virtuous as being just, having courage, being magnanimous, gentle, and wise. Though these qualities of a good person remain relevant today, we must remember that what qualifies as courageous, gentle, and so on, will depend on the audience's perceptions and beliefs.

   For example, during the 1992 presidential campaign, much controversy ensued over Bill Clinton's unwillingness to participate in the

Vietnam war a quarter of a century earlier. Clinton's position against the war was, for many, a sign of his weak moral character. He was, at best, weak and afraid; at worst unpatriotic. But for others, Clinton's willingness to go against the status quo in the name of a principle was a sign of his moral courage.

Beyond the knowledge and beliefs about the speaker that the audience brings to its interpretation of the communication, moral character can also be shaped through a speaker's use of language, structure, and reasoning. Jesse Jackson opened his speech at the 1996 Democratic Convention with a prayer for those public figures who had passed away since the last National Democratic Convention. He concluded the speech with a story about his father and his son while his family joined him at the podium. A man of God and a man of family is generally believed to be a moral man. In the case of Jesse Jackson, his moral character is often overshadowed by questions about his good will. Let us turn to this third quality of effective ethos.

Speakers with **good will** have their audience's best interests in mind. A speaker suggests good will by developing a relationship of trust, mutual admiration, openness, and honesty. Good will culminates in a rapport. Jesse Jackson's good will has been questioned because of his past actions and statements. His willingness to negotiate a Middle East peace agreement with the Palestinian Liberation Organization, his association with the Muslim leader Louis Farrakhan, and some derogatory remarks he made about the Jewish population in New York City have caused many Americans to distrust the Reverend Jackson. Jackson is a powerful speaker but his form and substance can be overshadowed by the audience's memories.

A speaker can attempt to change the preconceptions of the audience, present a case for good will, or both. Jackson's attempts to repair damaged ethos are generally unsuccessful, according to my classroom audiences of college students. The students' responses are always strongly divided. Many students, with little or no knowledge or beliefs about Jackson, become very enthusiastic about the man and his ideas after watching a video of him speak. Other students come to the video with a negative view of his ethos, although many of them have never heard Jackson speak. For these students, Jackson's lack of good will, suggested by their parents, teachers, and/or media (supertext) taints the meaning of his talk. What one group reads as caring, humble, charming, and convincing, others dismiss as insincere, over-dramatized, and manipulative.

A more successful image of good will is found in Jimmy Carter's campaign for the presidency in 1976. Television spots presented Carter's good will in the image of a common man. Carter, a wealthy plantation owner, was presented as a peanut farmer working his land. He was a man of the land, a man who got his hands dirty and felt physically tired at the end of a day. The audience is expected to reason from these images that "this is a man who would have our best interests in mind."[2]

The qualities of ethos were developed as a guideline for speakers. However, communication critics use these qualities to understand how audiences perceive a speaker's character. Actually, ethos is a concept that applies to directors, producers, writers, and creators of all forms of communication. The ethos implied in any communication text is an interplay of the good sense, morality, and good will that an audience attributes to a speaker. The speaker may intentionally build their ethos but the audience ultimately attributes ethos. Sometimes an audience will allow a speaker great latitude on good will if he or she excels in intelligence, or vice versa. As in all communication, there is no formula for being effective. A speaker must consider the entire communication context and so must the critic who unravels the construction of ethos. The following section illustrates how important it is for the critic to consider context.

▓▓▓▓ Critical Questions and Answers

Eric Weisman (1985) illustrates how ethos can be critically applied to contemporary communication. Among other insights, Weisman shows why audiences have attributed singer and songwriter Stevie Wonder with intelligence, strong moral character, and good will. Weisman uses more than Wonder's music to reconstruct the appeal of the singer's character. He locates much of Wonder's ethos in the contexts that surround and/or create his music.

1. Is the ethos effective in fulfilling the creator's purpose? Explain.

Critical comment on effectiveness: Most musicians attempt to improve their image. According to Weisman, Stevie Wonder is more concerned with serving good causes than his own image (p. 137). Wonder's genuine goodness plays a significant role in his universal appeal.

Wonder's intelligence is well-known to fans who have followed his career. Part of the fans' supertext is based on the way the 1960s media referred to Wonder as "the 12-year-old genius." By 1985, when Weisman wrote his critical essay, Wonder was widely recognized as one who overcame blindness and poverty in order to develop and share his enormous creative talent. In addition, he had received 14 Grammy Awards. Wonder's intelligence is solidified in his ability to play several musical instruments and to create socially and politically significant themes.

Wonder's goodness and good will, according to Weisman, are conveyed in his songs that celebrate American heroes and communicate faith in a supreme being and human spirituality. Wonder also conveys his goodness in public interviews that suggest he is humble and has a sense of humor about himself. Wonder's concern for others is found in his lyrics concerning "oppression, racial tension, and urban degradation" (p. 138). He celebrates American heroes of all skin tones and emphasizes the unity of all people. He was able to transcend the sociopolitical divisions of the sixties and continues to appear as a "lover of mankind" (p. 140).

2. Is ethos generated in ways that are truthful and ethical? Explain.

Critical comment on truth and ethics: Weisman concludes that Wonder's music "promotes timeless and universal philosophical truths. . . . genuine ideals" (p. 137). His lyrics inspire listeners to be better than they are.

3. How does ethos shape identities, ideas, and actions?

Ethos is most obviously a study of identity, in this case the character of a popular singer. According to Weisman, Wonder's character offers individual souls and a global audience an ideal version of itself as unified and loving. Wonder promotes a philosophy of cultural nationalism: "pluralism, peace, and universal oneness" (p. 149).

Aside from immersing himself in the historical context of Wonder's career, Weisman bases his study of ethos on the style of Wonder's lyrics and music. For instance, one of the ways Wonder promotes unity is that he includes singers and instruments from many countries and religions in his music. Weisman is also familiar with a vocabulary of structure as he combines his study of lyrics and music with form: "By mixing [via synthesizers] layer on layer of sound as a way of advancing his interfaith religious themes, Wonder makes use of a kind of auditory spiral or temporal mosaic form congruent with those themes" (p. 146).

Weisman's interpretive insights, typical of most critical studies of ethos, are directly connected to judgments about the truth and ethics of communication. Evaluating the ethics of communication is different from evaluating the speaker's ethos. Communication ethics entail questions about whether the speaker communicated correctly and fairly. One could create strong ethos but do so unethically. Weisman is more concerned with the truth in Wonder's music and does not explicitly address Wonder's ethics. We can assume, however, that unethical communication would reflect negatively on Wonder's ethos.

Let us conclude this chapter on ethos by emphasizing its significance in communication. Americans today seem to rely on ethos more than on other dimensions of meaning. Judging the character of, or behind, an idea is, perhaps, the best we can do in this information age. We often lack the knowledge, let alone the time, to consider the evidence and inferences in everyday meanings. We take the word of the auto mechanic that our car needs new brake shoes because he seems to know what he is talking about. We vote for a city council candidate because we read that she has a degree in economics and is raising a family. We select a physician based on recommendations from our friends, followed by the impressions we form during a 10-minute appointment.

Given its significance in meaning, it is important that we think critically about ethos. As we think critically about ethos, we should keep in mind that it is often difficult to attribute a message to one person. Certainly, your personal friends have an ethos, but much public communication involves a corporate, group, or cultural ethos. Ben and Jerry's ice cream stores and Eddie Bauer clothing stores have a corporate image. Does a film really belong to Martin Scorsese or an entire production team? So much of communication today is created by a team of experts who package ethos in the form of quick images and sound bites. Ethos remains a valuable concept, acknowledging that it no longer has a direct and uncomplicated reference to a person who speaks.

Notes

1. For a discussion of how Aristotle's statements on moral character evolved into theories of ethos, see Thonssen, Baird, and Braden (Chapter 14, 1970).

2. This sentence demonstrates how ethos entails reasoning. We reason from a speaker's behaviors—or from images of a speaker—to the claim that the speaker is believable.

14 Character as the Second Persona

The ethos of a speaker implies the ethos of an audience. Audiences participate in meaning by making the assumptions that are invited by the text of a speech, song, or joke. In this way, audiences implicate their own character. A part of my own character is revealed through a critical look at the meaning I took away from the film *Kids* (1995). The film is about kids, ranging in age from seven to fifteen, who are literally killing themselves through sex and drugs. The movie was shocking and sad. It is a hard movie for many people to watch. In discussing this movie with a friend, he pointed out that the main characters were Caucasian and asked if the movie would be so shocking and sad if it featured African American or Latino youths. I suspect the film would have had a different meaning. In other words, the effectiveness of the film may depend on some racist beliefs. The character of those who make sense of the film is called the second persona.

The concept of **second persona**, developed by Edwin Black (1970/1995), turns the idea of character onto the audience that makes sense of a text. *Persona* is often used by literary critics in reference to the speaker who is implied in a novel or poem. The second persona, according to Black, is the audience implied in any communication text. Unlike the concept of ethos, developed as part of a theory on how to speak effectively, the second persona was developed as a way to study the character of audiences who make sense of messages. In Black's words,

> The critic can see in the auditor implied by a discourse a model of what the rhetor would have his real auditor become. What the critic can find projected by the discourse is the image of a man [sic] and though that man [sic] may never find actual embodiment, it is still a man [sic] that the image is of. This condition makes moral judgment possible. (p. 192)

For Black, the second persona invites critics to judge the morality of the ideal audience. A study of ethos has the critic consider the speaker's moral character from the position of the audience. In comparison, a study of the second persona has the critic evaluate the audience's moral character through its assumptions and ideologies. The following section reviews some of the ways the concepts discussed in this book can lead the critic to the assumptions and ideologies of a second persona.

▨ The Ideology of the Ideal Audience

The second persona relates directly to the idea of "hailing" identities that was discussed in the first chapter. Simply put, hailing is the form of address we use when commanding someone's attention. When someone responds in a way that is fitting to the speaker's plan, then they must assume the subject position of a particular worldview. In a simple example, secretaries and students are often hailed by their first names, whereas professors are addressed more formally. Some professors will not respond to those who do not hail them according to the appropriate signifiers—"doctor," or "professor." There are, of course, social beliefs about social class, education, and work relationships that are assumed in these forms of address. The beliefs are affirmed, even enacted, through the use of these terms. In this chapter's opening illustration, the second persona of *Kids,* a viewer who is shocked and moved by the film, is a viewer who believes drug abuse and irresponsible sex are problems common to, expected, and even tolerated in minority teens but not white teens. It would be in keeping with the critical vocabulary to say the film hails a second persona. Since all meaningful communication requires participation from an audience, political speeches, comic routines, novels, and advertisements hail second personas.

The critic who unravels the second persona is most interested in the belief systems of the audience, or one who accepts the ideological position implied in communication. The critic pursuing the second persona uses any critical concept that will lead to a convincing ideological profile of the ideal audience. The critic can find the second persona in many places. The second persona is in language: the semiotics of the working class, cooking magazine *Elle* contains ideologies about food and fantasy (Barthes, 1980). The second persona is in structure: The narrative structure of farmers' stories identifies the myths of farming (Peterson, 1991). The second persona is in reasoning: The reasoning in Exxon's oil spill rhetoric entails ideologies of science and business (Sellnow, 1993).

The second persona inquires about the audience's ideology and then thinks about that ideology as identity. The second persona is a collective identity based on the ideology. Because the second persona may be, or may become, a real voice that influences social action, Black suggests it's important to judge the morality of the implied identity. Morality is the goodness of its character. The critical questions about moral character, raised in the previous chapter, inquire about the speaker's rhetorical choices. Within the framework of the second persona, we consider the morality of the audience's choices.

Critical Questions and Answers

The following summary and application of the second persona is based on Black's (1970/1995) study of those who were convinced by the rhetoric of the radical Right in the 1950s, 1960s, and 1970s. Black finds that the metaphor "communism is cancer" is used repeatedly by right-wing politicians but not used by those left of center. He focuses his study on the metaphors in the *Blue Book,* which, as the holy writ of the John Birch Society, informed the ideology of the radical Right. His method for laying out the metaphor is consistent with the vocabulary presented in Chapter 5. Communism is the tenor of the metaphor and cancer is the vehicle.

1. **Is the second persona effective in fulfilling the creator's purpose? Explain.**
   Critical comment of effectiveness: Black is not as concerned with the effectiveness of the *Blue Book* as he is with its ideological and moral

consequences. Black does, however, claim that the communism-is-cancer metaphor creates an audience that would effectively advance the political identity and agenda of the radical Right. The ideal audience is not inhibited by the possibility of war because it believes "the body-politic is already doomed, so that its preservation—the preservation of an organism already ravaged and fast expiring—is not really important" (p. 194). In short, an audience convinced of its impending destruction by the forces of communism might support policies that develop and use nuclear warfare.

2. **Does the second persona truthfully and ethically present ourselves, the world, and/or our ideas about ourselves and the world? Explain.**
   Critical comment on truth and ethics: Black concludes the second persona implied in communism-is-cancer metaphors is self-righteous, fanatical, suspicious, morbid, imprudent, and logically inconsistent. His justification for this moral judgment rests in the following explication of the ideology and identity of the second persona.

3. **How does the second persona shape identities, ideas, and actions?**
   Critical comment on identities, ideas, and actions: Black uncovers the ideology—hence identity, of the radical Right—by outlining the metaphorical transformations inherent in the metaphor.
   Cancer is believed be an illness that comes from within oneself rather than an illness that one catches from external sources; therefore, the metaphor appeals to those who may be ambivalent about their bodies and hold puritanical beliefs.
   Cancer is believed to be incurable; therefore, the metaphor induces its subscribers to risk everything, even nuclear war, to stop the spread of the disease.
   Cancer is believed to invade and grow in living organisms; therefore, the political state becomes a living being in which citizens see themselves as cells whose duty it is to fight off disruptive and disagreeable cells in order to save the state.
   Cancer is believed to be the work of a supernatural force, often a punishment for immoral behavior; therefore, believers of the metaphor are often religious fundamentalists.
   Cancer is believed to be the most terrifying disease known (to the audience in the 1950s and 1960s); therefore, one can only give in to it and die, or transcend oneself through religious faith.

Cancer is believed never to remain isolated for long, for it spreads through the entire body; therefore, believers assume that the presence of communists in this country will eventually contaminate us all.

Thinking critically about the second persona requires us to call on all of our critical skills. Black bases his critical evaluation on an interpretation of metaphors, but second personas take form wherever there are ideas and ideologies. The concept links what we believe to who we are and is therefore particularly useful for considering the moral character of our communication, ourselves, and our cultures.

One weakness in the concept is that it assumes the communication, under critical scrutiny, successfully creates the ideal audience. Audiences may resist intended meanings, and they may do so in ways that cannot be acknowledged. They could, for instance, ignore the metaphors or construct alternative meanings for them. Resistance will also suggest a persona. A related problem is that the second persona encourages the critic to consider the audience that is hailed in the communication. But what about the identity of those who are consistently ignored in communication? Recall that ignoring someone is a form of hailing. A good critic addresses the potential weaknesses of this concept by considering a plurality of second personas implied—and ignored—in communication.

15 Character as Identification

I identify myself in the mirror. I identify with an old man I pass on the street. I identify with female but not feminine. I identify with the rhythm of Jesse Jackson's oratory and Van Morrison's saxophone. **Identification** fits rather loosely into the dimension of meaning we are calling *character.* It is a much broader term than ethos or second persona. Identification is an ongoing process of establishing identity. Kenneth Burke (1969) is the scholar "identified" with the dramatistic perspective on communication and the concept of the pentadic drama discussed in an earlier chapter. He also developed the concept at hand. Burke defines the *identity* of something as "its uniqueness as an entity in itself and by itself, a demarcated unit having its own particular structure" (p. 21). Identification is the communication process through which we identify ourselves, the world, and our way of life. This chapter will elaborate on identification and its paradoxical nature. Next it will distinguish between identification, ethos, and the second persona. The chapter concludes with an illustration of how to think critically about identification.

An act of one person identifying with another means that they become joined in meaning—they are one, they are what Burke (1969) refers to as "consubstantial." He explains that "in being identified with B, A is 'substantially one' with a person other than himself" (p. 21). That is not to say that A and B are not distinct. Herein rests the paradoxical nature of identification. Every act of identification is an act of division.

It is through language that we identify and divide everything. People identify a supernatural universe and, in so doing, divide it from a natural universe. When we identify a chair, we divide it from all of the things that are not chairs. Language is also a tool for dividing ourselves into the conscious "I" who thinks about "me." Language divides us from one another interpersonally and socially, as it brings us together. We, for instance, identify nations that unite people under one term and simultaneously divide us from other nations.

This identification-division paradox is similar to the semiotic principle that the meanings of signifiers rest in their differences from one another. Burke's concept is broader, more philosophical and flexible than most semioticians' attention to differences. For Burke, identification and division are the origin and end of communication. The individual drive to identify the human condition is what, perhaps, motivates all meaningful communication. People are physically and psychologically separate and move toward identity as humans. Through identification, we establish and maintain social order. People are divided over issues that must be resolved by identifying their differences and working toward being of one mind and action. If identification becomes identity, there is no need for communication.

Identification is a more inclusive concept than either ethos or the second persona. All meaningful communication suggests the ethos of its creators and the persona of those who agree to participate, but not all components of every communication text are relevant to ethos or the second persona. However, all language identifies. Identification and division are umbrella concepts that include all of the ways people use symbols to establish and maintain order.

Forms of Identification

Critics working within Burke's dramatistic theory of communication consider how communication identifies human reality. The pentad, a concept discussed in the unit on structuring meaning, is Burke's concept for capturing the creation or identification of human dramas. A critic can, however, explore identification and division in any, or all, of the concepts presented here. Burke explains that people identify through "speech, gesture, tonality, order, image, attitude, [and] idea" (p 55). When a speaker uses style in such a way as to carry the audience along with the rhythm, the speaker and audience are said to have identified. When a speaker reasons and the audience fills in the necessary assumptions, we say they identify. The person who identifies with the corporate ethos of Eddie Bauer imagines him- or herself as successful but not pretentious, casual, and practical. My identification with my mother grows as I age and come to identify with more of her experiences.

In review, all meaningful communication is identification. Through the use of symbols, people move toward identity. As we come together in some ways, we come apart in others. The communication critic is interested in the symbolic forms of identification and their counterparts in division. Identification is always present, and a critic can easily use the concept with others. For instance, Eric Weisman's (1985) critical study of ethos outlined in the previous chapter, draws on Stevie Wonder's ability to *identify* with speakers and speeches of the past (p. 138), and to achieve "a consubstantial moment for blacks and whites throughout the world" (p. 139). The following section provides an extended example of a study that employs the concept of identification.

▨ Critical Questions and Answers

David Payne (1989) uses identification in combination with the concepts of narrative structure and psychological form to understand the ritualistic appeal of *The Wizard of Oz*. He points out that Americans of all ages have been watching this film yearly for 40 years. He examines several moments of consubstantiality between the film's structure and the psychological experience of the audience. Film and audience meet in psychological form. Form, the arousal and fulfillment of an audience's expectations, is a psychological process. The television audience that ritualistically watches Oz identifies the narrative form of the film with the psychological search for identity.

1. Is identification effective in fulfilling the creator's purpose? Explain.

Critical comment on effectiveness: Payne claims Oz is successful, in part, because it appeals to children and adults. Child viewers identify with Dorothy's powerlessness in her relationship with her stepparents and institutions. Dorothy must also do battle with the evil forces and natural disasters that occupy a child's mind. Dorothy's successful journey arouses and resolves the child's psychological anxieties because Dorothy comes home and it was all a dream. Adults who have experienced the adolescent quest for identity identify with Dorothy's journey.

All viewers may use the ritual to work on ongoing explorations into their identity. Borrowing from the contemporary philosopher Joseph Campbell's works on myths, Payne shows how Dorothy's journey to and from Oz is consubstantial with the archetypal myth of a hero who moves through three rites of passage. The hero must leave a secure world (separation), successfully overcome obstacles (initiation), and return home. This symbolic structure, found in cultures across time and space, suggests a psychological counterpart in form. The audience, according to Payne, "identifies" with this form regardless of age.

2. **Are the identifications truthful and are they ethically presented? Explain.**

   Critical comment on truth and ethics: Payne claims the identifications the audience makes with *The Wizard of Oz* are therapeutic in these times of individualism; thus, even though Payne does not say so, we could conclude the film serves an ethical function in our society. Furthermore, the form of the heroic quest, used in the narrative of *Oz*, advocates strong moral qualities: "courage, skill, and independence" (p. 38).

3. **How does indentification shape identity, ideas, and actions?**

   Critical comment on identity, ideas, and actions: The narrative form of *Oz* functions culturally as well as psychologically because it identifies our social beliefs, values, and practices at a particular time in history. Narratives function as cultural maps or guides through identity formation. *Oz* "foreshadows" young viewers' eventual quest for identity (Payne, pp. 32, 37). It also asks viewers to identify with traditional female social roles. Dorothy is the innocent who gathers the strength to nurture her puppy/baby—and the men she meets—on her journey into self-assertion. She does not initiate the action in her life. Evil challenges Dorothy's trusting, good nature. The evil neighbor, Elvira Gulch, threatens to take her puppy. A tornado sweeps Dorothy into a dream. Dorothy tries to obey the wicked witch by giving her the ruby slippers, but the shoes repel the touch of the witch. Dorothy fulfills a quest that is as trying as the quest of any man but resolves to remain on the farm away from the action (p. 35).

Payne's critical study illustrates the range of critical judgments but emphasizes the role of identification in establishing cultural ideologies and identity formation. The critic can also use identification to explore questions about the truth, ethics, and effectiveness of communication. Payne does not explicitly address questions about whether Oz is truthful or ethical, although we might say the psychological nature of identification "feels" truthful or real, and it advocates morals that are culturally valued.

Payne combines several critical concepts to study identification. He appraises the language, reasoning, and emotions of Oz, but does so within the framework of narrative form. Some critics have difficulty with the concept's spaciousness and flexibility. All meaningful communication is identification. And as a critical concept, it encompasses all other concepts. For these critics, the concept is not as analytical—or as pre-scriptive—as logical argument or ethos. For others, the concept's breadth makes it particularly viable and valuable. This chapter has only scratched the surface of identification. The concepts presented in the remaining chapters, dedicated to the emotional component of meaning, also describe forms of identification. I have introduced the concept in this unit on character because identification frames all communication as an act of giving the human condition meaning.

References For Unit V

Aristotle (1954). *Rhetoric*. (W. Rhys Roberts, Trans.). New York: Random House.
Barthes, R. (1980). *Mythologies*. (A. Lavers, Trans.). New York: Hill & Wang.
Black, E. (1995). The second persona. In C. Burgchardt (Ed.), *Readings in rhetorical criticism* (pp. 188-197). State College, PA: Strata Publishing. (Reprinted from *Quarterly Journal of Speech, 56*, 1970)
Burke, K. (1969). *A rhetoric of motives*. Berkeley: University of California Press.
Cohen, J. R. (1997). Poverty: Talk, identity, and action. *Qualitative Inquiry, 3*, 71-92.
Payne, D. (1989). *The Wizard of Oz:* Therapeutic rhetoric in a contemporary media ritual. *Quarterly Journal of Speech, 75*, 25-39.
Peterson, T. R. (1991). Telling the farmers' story: Competing responses to soil conservation rhetoric. *Quarterly Journal of Speech, 77*, 289-308.
Sellnow, T. L. (1993). Scientific argument in organizational crises communication: The case of Exxon. *Argumentation and Advocacy, 30*, 28-42.
Solomon, M. (1994). The rhetoric of dehumanization: An analysis of medical reports of the Tuskegee Syphilis Project. In W. Nothstine, C. Blair & G. Copeland (Eds.), *Critical questions: Invention, creativity and the criticism of*

discourse and media (pp. 301-322). New York: St. Martin's. (Reprinted from *Western Journal of Speech Communication, 49,* 1985)

Thonssen, L., Baird, A. G., & Braden, W. W. (1970). *Speech criticism* (2nd ed.). New York: Ronald Press.

Tonn, M. B., Endress, V. A., & Diamond, J. N. (1993). Hunting and heritage on trial: A dramatistic debate over tragedy, tradition, and territory. *Quarterly Journal of Speech, 79,* 165-181.

Weisman, E. R. (1985). The good man singing well: Stevie Wonder as noble lover. *Critical Studies in Mass Communication, 2,* 136-151.

UNIT VI

CRITICAL CONCEPTS THAT FOCUS ON EMOTION

According to Payne's (1989) critical interpretation of *The Wizard of Oz* (1989) discussed at the close of the previous unit, the structure of *Oz* is "emotionally healing" (p. 29). *Emotion,* the final component of meaning to be discussed, refers to the feelings revealed, used, and/or created in communication. Though feelings are believed to rest in a person's experiential truths, absolute values, and/or to be the result of chemical discharges in the brain, our critical interest is in how feelings are shaped by meaningful communication. The critic considers the emotional dimension of meaning as the interplay of the communication context and all of the components of meaning.

It is important for a critic not to sever emotion from the other dimensions of meaning, although historically, emotion has (along with character) been separated from rational meaning.[1] In everyday speech, we tend to suggest that emotion is distinct from, and even opposed to, reason. We might on occasion say, "I can't think straight, I am feeling too emotional," or "You have no evidence for your point, only emotion." Few, if any, scholars subscribe to the distinction between reason and emotion whole-heartedly. Emotion is interdependent with the other components of meaning and is therefore always present. And there are times when emotion dominates meaning and the critic will find a vocabulary for emotion necessary.

Emotional meaning can be critically understood through concepts presented in other chapters, a vocabulary of its own, or both. In this chapter, we will consider two concepts for thinking critically about the emotion in meaning. First, we will discuss **pathos** which has its roots in the classical study of rhetoric. Pathos was developed as a practical guide to speaking in order to elicit emotion but it can guide the critic through any form of communication. Second, we will look at the concept of **desire** as it is used by critics but developed by psychoanalysts and film theorists. Desire is particularly useful for understanding the emotional component of film, photography, and television.

■■■■■ NOTE

1. For a summary and bibliography of how the history of theories of communication have separated logic from emotion, intellect from feeling, understanding from will, and conviction from persuasion, see Thonssen, Baird, and Braden (1970), pp. 425-428.

16 Emotion as Pathos

Aristotle compared the emotional substance of communication to rhetorical argument and ethos. All three components of meaning are "artistic" ways of persuading another person. In artistic persuasion or proof, the resources for meaning are created by the communicators. They need not go to the library or the laboratory to acquire information but invent ideas from what is already believed or experienced. Rhetorical arguments, for instance, are based on widely accepted beliefs. Ethos is based on perceptions of intelligence, trustworthiness, and good will. **Pathos** is the neo-Aristotelian word for those components of meaning based on emotions.

Aristotle defined emotion as "all those feelings that so change men [sic] as to affect their judgments, and that are also attended by pain or pleasure" (p. 91). Eleven chapters in Book II of his *Rhetoric* are dedicated to the nature and causes of anger and calm, friendliness and hatred, fear and confidence, shame and shamelessness, kindness and unkindness, pity and indignation, envy and emulation. Aristotle's ideas on pathos continue to explain how people make meaning.

A contemporary critical study of cartoons, for instance, focuses on how political cartoons appeal to the public's fears that politicians are dishonest and opportunistic (Hill, 1978/1984). In the days before Jimmy Carter's election to the presidency, cartoons shaped the public's fear that he might base political decisions on his evangelical Christian beliefs. Such cartoons presented Carter in signifiers associated with Jesus Christ, angels, baptisms, and trickster healers. Though the American public believes its leaders should go to church, we do not want them to take religion too seriously (Hill, p. 188). In this chapter we will consider some of the many ways emotions are evoked, shaped, and/or manipulated.

Emotional Appeals

Aristotle made clear that an effective speaker makes use of all of the artistic forms of proof. That is, the speaker could create a convincing argument and a credible image of his character, as well as "put his hearers, who are to decide, into the right frame of mind" (p. 90). By "frame of mind," Aristotle is understood to be addressing human emotions. Human emotions can be thought of as organized along continua of intensity (Smith & Hyde, 1991, p. 450). For Aristotle, and a history of scholars to elaborate on his works, speakers evoke more intense emotions from audiences when the audience feels proximity to the subject of the emotion.[1] For instance, I will feel more pity for those whose town has been destroyed by a tornado if the town is physically near me or someone I feel close to. I will also feel more pity if I have been to the town. In addition to being physically and psychologically close to the topic, speakers can manipulate the intensity of emotion by making the audience believe the subject of emotion is close in time and plausibility. Speakers create emotional appeals and intensity through word choice, sentence structure, voice, gesture, organization, evidence, and inference. The speaker who wants the audience to identify with the pain of the tornado victims could compare the tragedy to a similar disaster that took place in his or her hometown. The speaker could state the statistical possibility of a tornado happening right here and now, or tell a personal story about a family member who lost everything in the tornado. Speakers who use pathos effectively, know the immediate emotional state of their audience and how to adapt emotional appeals and intensity to the particular situation.

Turning from the speaker to the critic who follows a neo-Aristotelian view of pathos, the critic should use whatever critical tools will facilitate an understanding of how emotions function in communication. In other words, a critic can study argument as a component of reasoning, as a component of pathos, or both. Here I will review the ways our present critical vocabulary lends itself to a critical study of pathos.

Language, whether we are talking about words, images, or any signifiers, arouses emotion through imagery, rhythm, associations, and connotations. The words and images portrayed in most cigarette advertisements are associated with the pleasures of pleasant weather, leisure time, friendships, and good health. The semiotic approach to language incorporates emotion into the second order signified, at which point a signifier becomes a culture's feelings and assessments about the first order signified. For instance, the Greek facade on the bank building conveys feelings of strength and security. Strength and security are feelings consistent with Aristotle's discussion of confidence as a pleasurable passion that can influence judgment. In this case, the passions associated with architecture might influence people to secure their money in the bank. Metaphors also commonly transform emotions from one idea to another. The fear of cancer, for instance, transfers to fear of communism in the statement "communism is spreading right here in our own country."

The psychological experience of "form" summarizes the important role the structure of communication has in emotional meaning. Structure, as organization, editing, narrative, or dramatic form, arouses and then soothes an audience's expectations. The traditional, neo-Aristotelian view of organization acknowledges the emotional influence of a speech that creates anxiety in the audience by establishing a problem, or a need for change, and then soothing the audience's concern by proposing a course of action. The arrangement of images in photography, film, or television, establishes the viewer's emotional relationship to the ideas on the screen. The editing of images in Frederick Wiseman's film *High School,* for instance, allows an adult audience to re-experience the tensions of parental and institutional authority (Benson, 1980/1984). Extreme close-up shots can convert objects of beauty and pleasure into unpleasant experiences, and vice versa. Similarly, through point-of-view shots, cameras can position the audience member inside a situation he would typically view from a distance and thereby make him feel uncomfortable.

Pathos is also intertwined with the construction of character in communication. Good will, one of the three qualities of good ethos, is, in a sense, an emotional bond between speaker and audience. People tend to attribute good will to those they perceive as being similar to themselves. And what better way to present oneself as similar to his or her audience than to identify with its emotions? One could hardly describe, let alone interpret and evaluate, the meanings generated at the 1996 Democratic

Presidential Convention without considering its attempts to identify with the public's emotions. The Democratic Party unabashedly presented itself as the party that identifies with pain. A chain of American citizens took turns behind a nationally televised podium telling stories of their personal economic collapse and recovery. Sarah and James Brady spoke about recovering from his brain injury and becoming advocates for gun control.[2] The actor Christopher Reeve, aided by a ventilator, spoke about his ongoing rehabilitation from a spinal cord injury and the importance of medical research. On a similar theme, Vice President Albert Gore talked about his sister's death from cancer. The emotional appeals described here attempted to identify with the audience and thereby generate the good will of the Democratic Party. They appealed to the audience's fear of illness and of losing a loved one. Given unaffordable medical costs, fear of illness comes with a fear of poverty. Ultimately, the audience member is to reason, "If the Democrats are similar to me, then their policies should exert good will toward me."

This last sentence reveals the connection between pathos and ethos, and pathos and reasoning. In this instance, the audience uses the emotional content of the Democratic platform (and its identification with it) to support a claim about the ethos of the Democrats. The statement, "If they feel as I do, then they will look out for my best interests," is the hypothetical inference that links evidence to claim. Not only do people reason from emotion but there are reasons for emotions.

Aristotle included thought as an essential cause of anger and fear. The thought of being outraged at someone causes anger, and the thought of being in danger causes fear.[3] Thoughts are reasons for our emotions. An antismoking campaign that presents a graphic photograph of a diseased lung and exclaims, "Don't smoke!" would strike one as an emotional appeal to fear. The fear is based on reasons: If you smoke, then you will die an unnatural death; I do not want to die an unnatural death, therefore I will not smoke.

In review, a critical study of pathos brings the emotional dimension of meaning into the foreground. A critical look at pathos includes the vocabulary of reasoning, character, structure, and language insofar as these components bear on the emotions. As is the case with all of the concepts for thinking critically about communication, critical insights into pathos depend on the critic's understanding of the communication situation. For instance, the feelings that an audience brings to a communication situation are as relevant to meaning as are its beliefs. Every dimension of the communication situation may interact with emotions.

The following illustration of how to use pathos as a critical tool is drawn from Robert Branham's (1991) study of the two antiabortion films *The Silent Scream* and *Eclipse of Reason*. Branham's study was also presented in the chapter on rhetorical argument as an illustration of how to critically evaluate evidence and inferences. Here we can see how the films' arguments include emotion and how argument and emotion depend on language, structure, and character.

▨ Critical Questions and Answers

Branham's critique of the reasoning in *Scream* and *Eclipse* lead him to conclude the films' arguments may effectively convince audiences to oppose abortion. But he dedicates the bulk of his critical evaluation to the films' misleading and unethical presentation of evidence. Branham's critique of pathos primarily addresses whether the films' emotional proof was effective. He shows how the films use of language, structure, and reasoning will emotionally persuade some of the audience and emotionally anger others.

1. **Does the speaker effectively use pathos to fulfill his or her purpose? Explain.**

Critical comment on effectiveness: The anti-abortion film *Eclipse of Reason* uses language and editing in the form of contrasting images to evoke the tensions between violence and love. The world of violence is depicted through such images as an atomic bomb, a starving child, the Ku Klux Klan, and a rock-throwing Palestinian youth, scored with ominous background music. Seven of the nine images used to portray the 'face of the world of love' show smiling children and have a sunny, musical accompaniment (p. 418).

The Silent Scream effectively uses evidence in the form of an emotional conversion narrative, which is common to the history of motion pictures and human experience. The evidence in the film is built around the testimony of people who converted from a prochoice to an anti-abortion stance. The familiarity of the tale/testimony arouses and satisfies the audience's expectations for this particular narrative structure. Branham explains the narrative structure and psychological form of the conversion experience:

> A parallel is thus constructed between the convert's transformative experiences and the viewer's experience of the film in which the convert's tale is recounted. . . . As the convert's tale progresses, the implied viewer is led down a parallel path from skepticism or alternative allegiance, through transformative experiences, and to some new commitment. (pp. 414-415)

The emotional content of the films can also account for their failure to persuade. The films attempt to evoke emotion through a bit of name calling. The films claim prochoicers "have resisted 'irrefutable' evidence," "are corrupt," and "are immoral." The prochoice viewer may be angered and insulted by the film (p. 424).

2. **Does the speaker use pathos ethically and truthfully? Explain.**

Critical comment on truth and ethics: Branham claimed the films' evidence was untruthful and unethical. The films' presentation of evidence did evoke emotions. In fact, according to Branham, the ambiguity of the evidence is key to the strong emotional appeal of *Silent Scream*: "The term 'late abortion' is used throughout the film to blur the differences between second and third trimester abortions. Images and examples of late abortions are drawn from the third trimesters; they are more shocking because the fetus appears more fully human and viable" (p. 416). Because the filmmakers distorted evidence to arouse emotion, we could say they made an unethical choice and that the emotion is based on false information.

3. **How does the use of pathos shape identities, ideas, and actions?**

Critical comment on identities, ideas, and actions: Though emotion may bring people together and increase human understanding, it often further divides the public on an issue. Branham claims the emotion in the films polarizes those who favor and those who oppose legalized abortions (p. 424). The films may increase the public's commitment to the issue but may not encourage its resolve.

Branham's critique reveals the interdependency of the components of meaning. He finds emotion in the films' use of language, evidence, and narrative form. In addition, studies of pathos, such as Branham's, lead us to understand how people shape identities, ideas, and actions. A few years ago, two professors of communication (Smith & Hyde, 1991) offered a reading of Aristotle that links the intensity of emotion to communal or public identity.[4] They claim that publics come into being and are sustained through emotional identification. People who identify at particular places on the continua of emotions become collectively identified in a psychological place, if you will. Returning to the example of the tornado, if you and I are both imagining and fearing the possibility of a tornado, then we will form (with others who have the same fear) a collective identity. In the case of the anti-abortion films, those who identify with the pleasure of the conversion tale and the pain of knowing viable fetuses are destroyed will identify with one another. The greater the intensity of their emotion, the more cohesive the group, because intensity is a matter of identification. According to Branham, these films invite collective identities to coalesce around intensely opposite emotional places.

Collective identities are necessary to concerted action in the form of social stability or social change. Therefore, the critical study of emotion can help us to understand action and inaction. The suggested relationship between identifying oneself as part of a public and social action is not the only connection between pathos and behavior. Emotions have long been considered the spark that moves people from thought to action. In the 17th and 18th centuries, faculty psychologists organized the human mind into faculties, typically distinguishing the faculty of understanding from the faculty of the will. According to George Campbell (1969), 18th century philosopher and rhetorician, one can incite an audience into action only by moving the will: "Passion is the mover to action, reason is the guide" (p. 78). We no longer separate the human mind into faculties, but contemporary theories of persuasion acknowledge that people are more likely to change their behavior if they experience some emotional stakes.

In sum, pathos, not unlike ethos and argument, is an inclusive concept. These three dimensions of meaning, which Aristotle called the three persuasive proofs, entail structure and language as well as each other. The problems inherent in using pathos as a critical guide to unraveling meaning are not unlike the limitations of the other concepts. It is at times too spacious. And it can be applied so narrowly as to ignore the feeling of thinking. The greatest advantage of pathos is that it works well with other critical concepts, including alternative ways of framing emotion.

Notes

1. Eighteenth century philosopher George Campbell (1969) elaborates on Aristotle's idea of proximity as intensifying the emotions in Chapter VII, Book I of his *Philosophy of Rhetoric*. Campbell's theory of emotions has influenced contemporary theories of communication, particularly the difference communication theorists draw between conviction and persuasion. Accordingly, conviction changes belief but persuasion changes behavior. Pathos is the essential link between the two (chap. IV & VII, Book I).

2. James Brady, Press Secretary under President Ronald Reagan, was wounded in an assassination attempt on the President.

3. For a discussion of the relationship between cognition and passion in Aristotle's works, see Fortenbaugh (1975).

4. Smith and Hyde link Aristotle's pathos to collective character through the philosopher Martin Heidegger's phenomenological theory of being.

17 Emotion as Desire

Some critics have found Sigmund Freud's psychoanalytic theory of pleasure a basis for studying communication. They claim the pleasures of reading a book or watching a movie are important to their meaning. Pleasure arrives with desire. **Desire** is a feeling of absence, or lacking. We desire what we do not have. We receive pleasure when the desirable gap is filled. Theories of desire and pleasure put the emotional dimension of communication into a psychoanalytic vocabulary. In psychoanalytic terms, desire is psychical, biological, social, and symbolic. As communication critics, we are most interested in the sociosymbolic forms of desire. We are specifically interested in how desire is shaped by, reflected in, and/or satisfied in communication.

One critical study, for example, explains how televised sports maintain an unfulfilled desire that draws sports fans to the games (Brummett & Duncan, 1990). According to its authors, television technology creates and satisfies a human desire to behold others through the use of close-ups and slow-motion replay. The words of the sports commentator create and please the desire to know and examine the athletes as if they are objects: the athletes' height, weight, marital status, and success and failure in the sport. The act of watching sports on television also feeds a desire to identify with the heroic athlete. In American society, men, more than women, are encouraged to identify with the images of athletes. Male and female spectators, however, are shaped into a communal identity of sports fans. The act of watching sports allows us to be one with others; we are together excited, concerned, dismayed, and ultimately pleasured by feelings of community. The feelings may not stay with us very long after the game but then there is always another game.

Most critical studies of meaning rooted in the concept of desire—as this one on desire in sport—are concerned with the symbolic construction of identities. The connection between desire and identity rests on Freud's psychosexual theory of development. Freudian desire is a psychosexual experience that originates in infancy, is repressed, and becomes part of the unconscious. The view of desire I am presenting is based on interpretations of Jacques Lacan's psychosocial theory of desire. Psychosocial desire is the drive to construct identity and ideology in language. Understanding desire as a psychosocial concept requires a basic outline of psychosexual desire. I will introduce a few key principles from Freud and Lacan's theories,[1] and then discuss the ways these principles can guide the critic through the pleasure of communication and its role in human identity and ideology.

Psychic Desires

Freud claims desire is born in infancy. The baby initially has no ego and identifies itself with its mother. The sense in which we use the word *identifies* is consistent with Burke's definition of identification. In fact, Burke's critical vocabulary can be synthesized with a psychoanalytical vocabulary, and we could say the baby is consubstantial with its mother.[2] The baby first experiences desire when he recognizes his own identity is separate or divided from his mother. Infants' desire for their mothers' milk, warmth, and comfort is associated with the pleasures of being consubstantial with the mother.

As a baby grows into a child, unfulfilled desire for the mother directs the child's search for identity. The child learns to repress the desire for the mother if he is to function socially. At the moment of repression, the child becomes split between the unconscious desire for the pleasures associated with infancy and the conscious desire to follow the rules of society. Repressed desire often reveals itself in the imaginary realms of dreams and fantasies.

At this point in our discussion, we have reviewed the elements of Freud's theory necessary to understanding psychosocial desire.[3] As we move into a discussion of psychosocial desire and its value as a critical concept, keep in mind the pleasures of being an uncomplicated, pre-identified infant and the subsequent desire for identity.

Freud's theory must be adapted to meet the goals of the communication critic. Most important, we must move the psyche into language. Jacques Lacan, a French psychoanalyst, used many of Freud's ideas to create a theory of identity in language, or what Lacan calls "subjectivities." Lacan puts Freudian consciousness, identity, and desire in language. It is Lacan's more psychosocial view of desire that has influenced critics, particularly film and literary critics. We can adapt theories of desire to understanding the emotional content of much communication.

Lacan, similar to Freud, believes babies do not initially distinguish themselves from their mothers, and that this experience of consubstantiality is pleasurable. Babies are not consciously divided from others, the world, or even themselves. Initially, a baby looks into a mirror or at another person and perceives himself. According to Lacan, the moment the baby acknowledges the division between himself and that image of himself (the imaginary self) is the moment of self-consciousness. It is also the moment in which a child first acquires language necessary to functioning in the social world. The image is the baby's first experience with language.

The moment of self-consciousness in either Freud or Lacan's terms is the first moment of desire, a moment marked by the deficiency of what we are not. Freudian consciousness begins when the baby represses his desire for his mother. Human identity is born in the split between a struggle for the pleasures of the unconscious and the social constraints imposed on the individual. Lacanian consciousness begins during the "mirror stage," when the baby recognizes himself as an entity separate from others. Human identity is born in the split between the image and the child who is conscious of perceiving the image. The language of the image identifies the infant and yet is separate from it.

Lacan believes the child enters language with images, but all language, whether mirrors, dreams, or words, create, and maintains a schizophrenic identity: I am that image in the mirror but I am not. *I* can be *me* and consider myself as *she*. Lacan calls identity created in language, "split-subjectivity." Terry Eagleton (1996), a contemporary literary theorist and critic, summarizes the language-identity predicament: "To enter language, then, is to become a prey to desire. . . . To enter language is to be severed from what Lacan calls the 'real', that inaccessible realm which is always beyond the reach of signification, always outside the symbolic order" (p. 145). Language is always a movement or tension between what is and what is not. If human identity is in language, then it also must move between what is and what is not.

Lacan's theory that language creates split subjectivities has attracted communication critics because it places human language at the center of all meaning, including what it means to be human. It is not a stretch, therefore, to say Lacan's theory grants communication critics an important role as social watch dogs. The fundamental rupture that we call human consciousness makes all people vulnerable to communication, which fills the void. Identity and ideology are the medicine for desire. A more obvious example of the human desire for identity being soothed in communication is found in people persuaded into the belief systems of religious cults. The cult supplies the desiring subject with a seamless identity within a system of beliefs about how the world is. In less obvious ways, all cultural meanings have a stake in desire. Ideologies are pleasurable because they smooth over the divisions inherent in language and all that humans experience through language.

Human beings can never avoid identity and ideology, nor would we want to because we desire the orderly pleasures they offer us. We can become more critical of the meaningful choices we make. Critics have developed myriad ways of using desire as a critical tool. I am presenting only one of many renditions of desire in meaning.

The critic under the influence of Lacanian desire asks how the viewer, listener, reader, or audience is positioned in and by language. The question can be answered through a combination of concepts presented in previous chapters. The vocabularies of narrative, editing, and semiology are most commonly used as tools for probing the workings of desire. It makes sense that these concepts should prevail, given the influence that psychoanalytic theories of desire have had on film and literary critics.

A critic can interpret the nature of desire in meaning through a study of style or metaphor. But critical studies of desire typically define language broadly, through semiotics. Semiotics invites critics to view theme parks (Giroux, 1994; Gottdiener, 1995) movies (Giroux, 1994; Pribram, 1988) and shopping malls (Gottdiener, 1995; Morris, 1993), as giving pleasure in the form of identity. Using the vocabulary of style, metaphor, or semiology, the critic studies the ways language hails audiences and interpellates them into ideology.

The vocabulary of editing is also a tool for studying psychoanalytic desire because of its focus on images. Film theorists claim film audiences re-experience the pleasures of being a baby fixated on its image in the mirror. In other words, the feeling of losing yourself in a film imitates the preconscious unity of identity. The pleasures are temporary, for every act of identification is an act of division. Even when lost in a film, you will recover yourself watching the film (Flitterman-Lewis, 1987, p. 182). Using the vocabulary of editing, the critic studies the ways the production of shots, scenes, and sequences positions the viewer to identify with the film.

Narrative structure is particularly useful for interpreting how film, literature, and much of television position the audience. It can be used with a vocabulary of semiotics and editing to understand the subjectivities of the audience. Narratives use narrators, characters, and point of view to position the audience.

E. Ann Kaplan (1988) draws on the vocabulary of editing and narrative to illustrate how Madonna's music video, *Material Girl* (1985), plays on its young female audience's unsatisfied desire for identity. The video is based on a well-known dance sequence in the 1953 film *Gentlemen Prefer Blondes*. The film, in what was typical filmmaking in 1953, is a story about women in search of wealthy husbands. The semiotics and editing of the film are framed from a male point of view. That is, most shots frame women as they are being viewed by men. Madonna's video imitates a film scene in which Marilyn Monroe sings and dances for the male gaze of the audience. The audience includes the man who is watching Monroe in the narrative, as well as the audience viewing the narrative from the position of his male gaze. In contrast to the unified male gaze of the film's narration, Madonna's video invites viewers to identify with many gazes, including gazes that critique the male gaze. It does so through strategies of editing and narrative.

The narrative in the video involves multiple Madonnas. The audience is aware of a "real" Madonna that made the video. The story she tells is about Madonna #1 who stages a performance within the narrative, as well as the character of Madonna #2 who is Madonna #1 performing within the narrative. Madonna #1 and #2 are shown in various settings: the stage, a film of a performance on the stage, backstage, a dressing room, and outside the studio. Because the video is based on a film, these characters also refer to the mythic character of Marilyn Monroe.

The framing and editing of shots in the video are often ambiguous and allow viewers to position themselves in a variety of gazes and roles. For instance, the video opens with a classic male gaze. There is a close-up of a director, and then shots of a film starring Madonna. Another close-up of the director "with an obsessed glazed look on his face" cements his desire for the woman in the film. The camera then cuts to a shot of the director and another man sitting in front of the film starring Madonna. The camera moves into a close-up of Madonna's face, looking seductively at the camera and then at the men sitting around her. Suddenly the perspective and setting have changed from a male gaze looking at a film of Madonna #1 to being in the film as Madonna #2 (pp. 141-142). This is just one example of how subject position changes. *Material Girl* continues in the vein of shifting characters, settings, and ultimately point of view so that the female audience can identify with being seductive, feminine, gutsy, and independent. According to Kaplan, the narrative and editing technique of MTV often "reproduces the decentered human condition that is especially obvious to the young adolescent" (p. 137).

In review, critical interpretations of desire ask how communication arouses and/or satiates desire by positioning the audience as a subject in the communication. Some concepts are more useful than others for pursuing the role of desire in meaning. Those who use psychoanalytic theories to study communication typically employ some combination of the concepts presented here. Whatever interpretive path a critic takes to desire, he or she will eventually arrive at evaluation. The following critical study of the desires and pleasures of walking and shopping the streets of a refurbished historical town summarizes how people locate themselves in language.

Critical Questions and Answers

You probably do not think of places as communication texts. A street corner is not a billboard. Sitting in a cafe drinking coffee is not sitting in a theatre watching a film. And yet, places are constructed of meaningful signifiers. The glass-encased cakes at the cafe, and the cloth napkins, identify the place as refined. These signifiers position the people who look at the cafe and/or go into the cafe. The cafe, then, can be seen as a communication text.

Greg Dickenson (1997) takes Old Pasadena, a refurbished town in the Los Angeles area, as his communication text. His study begins with an analysis of the context: The people who cruise through Old Pasadena on foot, or in an automobile, have fragmented identities, brought about by fast-paced, technologically advanced, post-industrial urban life. People no longer live with, or often near, their families. There is no longer a sense of community. These people make up the audience of Old Pasadena. Dickenson frames the audience in the vocabulary of desire. The audience, being mostly middle-class locals and tourists, lack historical continuity, a sense of belonging, and identity. According to Dickenson, the semiotics of Old Pasadena's architecture provides the public with memory in the form of a narrative history. The semiotics of Pasadena provides the town's visitors with identities and ideologies.

1. Does the use of desire effectively fulfill the creator's purpose? Explain.

Critical comment on effectiveness: Old Pasadena does provide contemporary visitors with a wide range of coherent and stable identities through the landscape, signs and architecture. The combination of signifiers creates a nostalgic place to be that draws on myths of an earlier time of comfort and community. Historical sites offer a sense of material continuity. The road signs and banners present a story of history: "Old Pasadena," "This is the historic Route 66," "This building was once a livery, then a Texaco station, and now a shopping center that is a gateway to the past." The style of the buildings and streets has been "restored" to imitate historical styles from Spanish Colonial to 1950s America. "These different nostalgic strategies . . . provide a message of personal and collective memories." Each nostalgia "sets in motion the desire for a unified and unifying past" (p. 15). Historical signifiers suggest that this place was here, is here, and the visitor can feel grounded in being here. Visitors can choose to enact their identities through consuming the sites, the images, and the goods that are sold in Old Pasadena.

2. Is desire used ethically and truthfully? Explain.

Critical comment on truth and ethics: There are some issues of truth and ethics relevant to the memories and identities constructed in Old Pasadena. First, whereas the town promises a unified nostalgia, it represents a montage of pasts and denies the "possibility for any singular and meaningful past" (p. 15). Old Pasadena does not deny the split subjectivities of the visitors but appeases them into fragmented bits of history. The histories presented are devoid of their own ruptures. For instance, the clothing store, Banana Republic, can be easily associated with 19th century imperialism, yet it ignores the violent and oppressive relationship between the colonizer and the colonized.

The identities that visitors enact in this so-called historical place are very stylized as well. According to Dickenson, "These alleys and squares are designed for people to wander, browse, sit and watch, to promenade, to see and to be seen. None of these things are done without thought to the way one looks, to the way the body will be seen. In these spaces, so conveniently provided, individuals continually perform themselves" (p. 16).

Dickenson does conclude that Old Pasadena and sites of memory "as commercialized, sanitized and repressive as they are—are, nevertheless, compelling responses to deeply troubling contemporary problems" (p. 22).

3. How does desire shape identities, ideas, and actions?

Critical comment on identities, ideas, and actions: People proclaim and perform their identities in Old Pasadena. Old Pasadena does not determine how people will identify themselves but influences their choices for creating identities. The signifiers of Old Pasadena do not help people to "find" themselves, but allow them a more active and performative role in "identifying" themselves (p. 19). In the act of identifying themselves in Old Pasadena, people turn themselves into part of the site. They are aesthetic objects to be looked at. "People become billboards, signs advertising the style and the wares of the site" (p. 16).

Dickenson's critical insights make use of a variety of concepts presented in this book, but desire for identity is the concept that frames his interpretation of Old Pasadena. Old Pasadena effectively plays on the contemporary visitors' desire for a continuous identity. It soothes the ruptures of identity with ideologies that range from the superiority of western society to idyllic smalltown America. Evaluating the truth of psychosocial desire is paradoxical. According to the psychoanalytic view, humans are split-subjects in search of a unity that can never be. The truth is there is no *one* identity. If communication effectively pleasures desire, then it must cover or hide ruptures that are natural to human consciousness. The critic interested in the truth of desire assumes some distortion or tension and seeks out the ways language covers the ruptures and contradictions. Old Pasadena does this by creating times and places that never were.

In review, psychoanalytic desire is a concept that critics use to interpret and evaluate the emotional dimension of meaning. Because desire is born with consciousness, it is also very much about identity. I have included desire in this unit of emotion rather than character, which is also very much about identity, because it focuses on the psychic pain and pleasures of meaning.

The vocabulary of desire is quite complex and critics apply the concept in a great range of ways. My explanation of the concept has avoided some key problems inherent in much psychoanalytical criticism. Some critics may assume, with Freud and Lacan, that all people, regardless of their lifetime or cultural identities develop in the same way. Critics using the psychoanalytic vocabulary also often ignore the power of the audience. The examples that I presented in this chapter assume audiences have some choices in how they are positioned. My examples also assume that the split subjectivities of the audience makes multiple identities possible. The female MTV viewers can identify with several images of femininity. The visitors to Old Pasadena have a selection of signifiers from which to shape their identities. As previously stated, the impossibility of grasping a real identity makes the question of truth a paradox. It is a paradox a critic resolves by revealing the contradictions, ruptures, and inconsistencies concealed by ideology. The critic reveals our desire to us.

Notes

1. Basic summaries of how Freud and Lacan's psychoanalytic theories are used in communication criticism are to be found in C. Belsey (1988, chap. 4); T. Eagleton (1996); and S. Flitterman-Lewis (1987). There are many ways in which Freud and Lacan's theories have been interpreted and adapted for critical communication studies. My rendering of desire in this chapter has been influenced by an amalgam of feminist responses to Freud and Lacan. The feminist readings of psychoanalytic desire are best summarized in E. A. Kaplan (1987) and J. Byars (1988).

2. One can give Burke's dramatistic theory a psychoanalytic reading. I have discussed Burke's concepts (form, identification, division, pentad) in other chapters because they need not be read as a psychoanalytic theory.

3. My brief outline of Freud avoids the points at which Freud becomes more controversial. For Freud, identity is initially and essentially pleasurable and sexual.

The baby girl and the baby boy embark on different paths of identity, and this is the subject of much feminist debate. Also, see note 1.

▨ Reference List For Unit Six

Aristotle (1954). *Rhetoric.* (W. Rhys Roberts, Trans.). New York: Random House.

Belsey, C. (1988). *Critical practice.* New York: Methuen.

Benson, T. (1984). The rhetorical structure of Frederick Wiseman's *High School.* In M. Medhurst & T. Benson (Eds.), *Rhetorical dimensions in media* (pp. 80-111). Dubuque, IA: Kendall/Hunt. (Reprinted from *Communication Monographs, 47,* 1980)

Branham, R. J. (1991). The role of the convert in "Eclipse of Reason" and "The Silent Scream." *Quarterly Journal of Speech, 4,* 407-426.

Brummett, B., & Duncan, M. C. (1990). Theorizing without totalizing: Specularity and televised sports. *The Quarterly Journal of Speech, 76,* 227-246.

Burke, K. (1969). *A rhetoric of motives.* Berkeley: University of California Press.

Byars, J. (1988). Gazes/voices/power: Expanding psychoanalysis for feminist film and television theory. In E. D. Pribram (Ed.), *Female spectators: Looking at film and television* (pp. 110-131). London: Verso.

Campbell, G. (1969). *The philosophy of rhetoric.* (L. Bitzer, Ed.). Carbondale: Southern Illinois University Press.

Dickenson, G. (1997). Memories for sale: Nostalgia and the construction of identity in Old Pasadena. *The Quarterly Journal of Speech, 83,* 1-27.

Duffy, M. & Gotcher, M. J. (1996). Critical advice on how to get the guy: The rhetorical vision of power and seduction in the teen magazine YM. *Journal of Communication Inquiry, 20,* 32-48.

Eagleton, T. (1996). *Literary theory: An introduction.* Minneapolis: University of Minnesota Press.

Flitterman-Lewis, S. (1987). Psychoanalysis, film, and television. In R. C. Allen (Ed.), *Channels of discourse* (pp. 172-210). Chapel Hill: University of North Carolina Press.

Fortenbaugh, W. W. (1975). *Aristotle on emotion.* New York: Harper and Row.

Giroux, H. A. (1994). *Disturbing pleasures.* New York: Routledge.

Gottdiener, M. (1995). *Postmodern semiotics: Material culture and the forms of postmodern life.* Cambridge, MA: Blackwell.

Hill, A. (1984). The Carter campaign in retrospect: Decoding the cartoons. In M. Medhurst & T. Benson (Eds.), *Rhetorical dimensions in media* (pp. 182-203). Dubuque, IA: Kendall/Hunt. (Reprinted from *Semiotica, 23,* 1978)

Kaplan, E. A. (1987). Feminist criticism and television. In R. C. Allen (Ed.), *Channels of discourse* (pp. 211-253). Chapel Hill: University of North Carolina Press.

Kaplan, E. A. (1988). Whose imaginary? The television apparatus, the female body and textual strategies in select rock videos on MTV. In E. D. Pribram (Ed.), *Female spectators: Looking at film and television* (pp. 132-156). London: Verso.

Morris, M. (1993). Things to do with shopping centres. In S. During (Ed.), *The cultural studies reader* (pp. 295-319). London: Routledge.

Payne, D. (1989). *The Wizard of Oz:* Therapeutic rhetoric in a contemporary media ritual. *Quarterly Journal of Speech, 75,* 25-39.

Pribram, E. D. (Ed.). (1988). *Female spectators: Looking at film and television.* London: Verso.

Smith, C. R. & Hyde, M. J. (1991). Rethinking 'the public': The role of emotion in being-with-others. *Quarterly Journal of Speech, 77,* 446-466.

Solomon, M. (1994). The rhetoric of dehumanization: An analysis of medical reports of the Tuskegee Syphilis Project. In W. Nothstine, C. Blair & G. Copeland (Eds.), *Critical questions: Invention, creativity and the criticism of discourse and media* (pp. 301-322). New York: St. Martin's. (Reprinted from *Western Journal of Speech Communication, 49,* 1985)

Thonssen, L., Baird, A. G., & Braden, W. W. (1970). *Speech criticism* (2nd ed.). New York: Ronald Press.

Tonn, M. B., Endress, V. A., & Diamond, J. N. (1993). Hunting and heritage on trial: A dramatistic debate over tragedy, tradition, and territory. *Quarterly Journal of Speech, 79,* 165-181.

Weisman, E. R. (1985). The good man singing well: Stevie Wonder as noble lover. *Critical Studies in Mass Communication, 2,* 136-151.

UNIT VII

DEVELOPING CRITICAL POWERS

It is difficult to bring closure to a process that we have just begun. It is also difficult to conclude, because the vital role of communication in shaping our lives requires an ongoing critical attitude. The "concluding" chapter will, therefore, summarize key ideas and offer a glimpse of what we do not yet know. I will review the critical concepts for unraveling the role of language, structure, reasoning, character, and emotion in meaning. I will do so by putting them into a philosophical, or what we might call meta-critical, context. Philosophical thinking is thinking about our critical thinking. Specifically, this final chapter examines the assumptions made by communication critics. The assumptions, stated and implied throughout the pages of this book, justify critical thinking. It is time to look at them more closely.

The role of communication in identity, knowing, and action was the subject of the first chapter. There, at the beginning, it was enough to say that communication shapes who we are, what we know, and what we do. The word *shapes* includes the possibility that communication creates and reflects reality simultaneously. The word *reality* encompasses all of the dimensions of our lives presented in the first chapter: our individual and social identities, our perceptions and ideas about the world, and our individual and social actions. The second chapter claimed that thinking critically about communication gives one power in identity, knowing, and action. The critical vocabulary, presented in the remaining chapters, was justified on the basis of these claims. The final chapter examines some of the theoretical assumptions we make when we claim that components of meaningful communication are inseparable from reality.

As we address the assumptions that critics make, we move to yet another level of thinking. This book is about communication and how to think critically about communication. We now examine our critical thinking. The reflective process of examining our own vocabulary is really the final phase of critical thinking. It should ensure that critical thinking has no final phase.

18 Critical Powers Over Who We Are, What We Know, and What We Do

The doing of criticism is an individual thing. . . . Moreover, a given critic may be interested in one sort of text on Monday and a different sort on Wednesday. Likewise, critics change their modes of operation from project to project since sterility means the death of criticism. The best critic chooses the right way to examine the right text.

Hart, 1994, p. 77

Critical thinking has no final phase but it does have many potential starting points. Sometimes we initiate the critical process with a judgment, unsupported with analysis and interpretation. At other times we have a curious or practical interest in a communication text (a movie) or context (the civil rights movement). Critical thinking often begins, and should always lead to, a particular question or goal. For instance, in a legal case, we might ask whether a defendant's words reflect truth. If we are interested in how a film could influence children, then we begin by asking about the effects of communication. Wherever you begin the critical thinking process, the "right way to examine the right text" is to reflect on your own assumptions and goals and use concepts for interpreting meaning that are consistent with them.

This chapter is organized around four assumptions common to critical thinking. I believe that most critics employ most or all of these assumptions at sometime or another. All of the assumptions address the relationship between language, identity, knowing, and/or action. Language is our foundation because it is the most basic component of communication and criticism. Structure, reasoning, character, and emotion entail language and so we will consider these concepts as they relate to assumptions about language. Each section concludes with a discussion of how a critic, thinking within the framework of the assumption, may find more choice and power in meaning.

Language Influences Social Action

The classical study of rhetoric was developed around the belief that language influences social action. The citizens of Athens saw public communication as essential to democracy. Democratic policy making and legal decisions cannot be determined with certainty, and so we must persuade one another to agree with our opinions. It is through rhetoric, or persuasive communication, that publics form and affect social action. Writing approximately 2,400 years ago, Isocrates asserts the significance of public speech to democratic life in particular and human existence in general:

> Because there has been implanted in us the power to persuade each other and to make clear to each other whatever we desire, not only have we escaped the life of wild beasts, but we have come together and founded cities and made laws, and invented arts; and, generally speaking, there is no institution devised by man which the power of speech has not helped us to establish. . . . Through [the power of speech] we educate the ignorant and appraise the wise; for the power to speak well is taken as the surest index of a sound understanding, and discourse which is true and lawful and just is the outward image of a good and faithful soul. (Translated by Norlin, 1956, p. 328)

Few would disagree that language influences social action; therefore, most critical concepts can be more or less useful in the service of this assumption. Aristotle's theory of rhetoric developed as a study of how language can and does influence social action; therefore, the neo-Aristotelian concepts—*style, organization, rhetorical argument, ethos,* and *pathos*—are fundamental to understanding how communication influences people to act.[1] The other concepts presented in the pages of this book can also guide the critic through thinking about the ways language influences action. They can be used with or without the vocabulary of traditional theories of rhetoric. The compatibility of concepts will depend on what other assumptions the critic is making.

Critical Powers

When you realize the potential of language to influence behavior, you can use your critical insights to influence others and to protect yourself from undue influence. Because the classical approach was developed as a practical model, it lends itself to questions about a speaker's effectiveness. You gain some power in your interaction with others when you understand how people are influenced by communication. The traditional concepts also implore critical thinkers to evaluate the truth of evidence and the ethical implications of ideas. A teacher of mine, Gordon Hostettler (1980), reminds us that today, or centuries ago, "armed with knowledge of rhetoric we are better able to combat demagoguery and chicanery; ignorant of it we may stand powerless before them" (p 340).

Those groups who have power in and over communication have social power. A group gains social power when their meanings and ways of making meaning are assumed to be natural by the most people. Recall that cultural groups become dominant when powerful agents of socialization, such as media, government, and education, assume their view of the world and hail all others according to that view. Being an active participant among these communication power struggles is necessary to a participatory democracy. Critical thinking is one way to be active in meanings that influence action.

Language Expresses Identity

Language is an expression of human identity. According to this assumption, people exist and have meaning independent of, and prior to, language. People use language to reveal their identities to others. In other words, I have an identity and my words, my signifiers, including clothing and facial expressions, are an extension of who I am. We make this assumption when we are enamored with a musician we believe is behind the music, or when we struggle for the "right" words to express ourselves. We often assume an identity beneath language when we question another's sincerity, honesty, and ethics of communication.

Several of the critical concepts that we have addressed work well with the assumption that language expresses the human psyche, human experience, or individual and cultural character. *Style,* as conceived by the neotraditionalists, encompasses a person's personality or attitude toward life. To describe the 1992 Independent presidential candidate Ross Perot's style as straightforward and simple is to say something about Ross Perot the individual. Theories of style say language is more than a study of words; it is also a study of the psychology of the person or persons who create communication. Accordingly, a study of style can also be a study of *ethos.* Does the speaker's style reveal an honest, intelligent, and moral person?

Some *Metaphors* are believed to be rooted in human experience and may be critically considered as expressions of identity. Orientational metaphors, such as up-down, in-out, front-back, may have a basis in our physical experiences. For example, consciousness is up in "get up," "wake up," and "he rises early." Unconsciousness is down in "he fell asleep," "he dropped off to sleep," and "he's under hypnosis." These metaphors may be rooted in an existential reality that "humans and most other mammals sleep lying down and stand up when they awaken" (Lakoff & Johnson, 1980, p. 15). Archetypal metaphors, those found across time and cultures, are often grounded in four natural sources: light and darkness, the sun, heat and cold, and the seasons, thus expressing the universal experiences of human existence (Osborn, 1967). If some metaphors originate in natural experiences, then they may express a natural or fundamental human identity.

Semiotics does not address itself to anything outside of language and therefore does not lend itself to the expressive view of language as I have been discussing it. The expressive view suggests that an identity is first present and then expressed. But there are different views of expressionism and semiotics, and most would accept that semiotics expresses cultural identities.[2]

Most of the critical concepts presented in this book can be compatible with the assumption that language is an expression of human experience. For instance, theories on *emotions* and communication assume that language extends or expresses one's emotional state or desire for identity.

Similarly, the rhythm and pacing of *editing* or a *narrative* structure can be viewed as expressions of human experience, in which the *form* of the communication "rings true."

Critical Powers

A critical thinker who assumes the expressive nature of language will often use critical concepts as a mirror for identities—to reveal who we were then, who we are now, or who they are. Such knowledge of ourselves and others increases empathy. I believe empathy is in itself valuable, but in keeping with the theme of this book, I note that empathy also enhances one's ability to be part of a community that is active in determining what things mean.

When communication is deemed expressive, there is often the expectation that it reveals the truth about human experience or the individual character behind language. Most communication critics are not as interested in pursuing an essential identity "behind" communication as they are interested in the identities represented or created in communication, especially when the critical purpose is, as ours is here, to gain power over the kinds of people we are. Even if we believe there is an essential identity behind some, or all, language, there is little critical thinking could do to change that identity. As critics of communication, we are confined to reading identity through language.

Language Represents Ideas About Ourselves and the World

You can accept language as an expression of identity and also assume that language sometimes represents ideas about who we are. *Ideas* is a key word in this assumption, for it joins who we are to what we know. Knowing, broadly defined, is having ideas in the form of beliefs, attitudes, values, and ideologies. According to this representational view, language represents ideas that are formed in a person—often called the subject—about objects in the world. Objects of knowing include physical things like chairs, social policies such as the welfare system, and even people, such as the subject who knows. In other words, the process of having ideas about one's self and others (identities) is the same process as having ideas about things (knowing). Regardless, our focus is on language, which in either case represents ideas. Let us consider how some concepts work with the assumption that language is representative.

Style, semiotics, and *metaphors* can frame language as representative of ideas. The principal difference between the representational and expressive assumptions is that the former acknowledges a gap between language and who we are. Under the expressive assumption, style reveals character to us. The representational gap is where the audience and the critic actively participate in the construction of meaning. The critic who recognizes the gap is on his way to discovering "possible" identities. Under this assumption, a critical view of how language represents *ethos* directs the critic to identify the character of the speaker as the audience would. If we are interested in the ethos of a controversial rap music artist, we must acknowledge that sociocultural groups interpret the artist's signifiers differently. People do not agree on what represents good character. Different cultures most certainly represent the characteristics of good ethos—intelligence, morality, and good will—differently. When we acknowledge that there is a gap between language and the identity it represents, we open ourselves to a range of potential meanings where there was once only one. Because we do choose our meanings, we can be held accountable for them.

The second persona can be viewed from the representational assumption, and it reminds critics that language implicates the audience who goes along with the representation of ideas. We implicate ourselves when we sit among friends who are regaling in racist, sexist, or ethnic humor.

In addition to those concepts relating specifically to identity, *organization* and *editing* can be understood as representing the structure of thought; *narratives* are particularly useful to understanding how people structure ideas about themselves and others; *rhetorical argument* is a concept that considers how people combine old ideas into new ones. *Field-dependent reasoning* can do the same but directs the critic to consider the ideas that regulate the combination of ideas into reasoning.

<h2>▨ Critical Powers</h2>

Critics are bound to confront questions of truth and ethics when they think under the influence of the representational assumption. Whereas expressive language is a natural extension of a person or humanity, representative language is often an arbitrary, social construction of an idea.[3] There are different kinds of representationalism but they all open spaces between the subject who uses language, the ideas that are represented in language, and the things that are represented in language. The representational view, therefore, often separates knowing from knowledge and beliefs from true knowledge.

The critical vocabulary presented here offers different notions of truth as well as standards for evaluating truth. Critics can use *style* to ask if language accurately represents a person, the world, or both. *Rhetorical argument* invites questions about the accuracy of evidence. *Field-dependent reasoning* suggests we turn to the fields of argument for definitions and standards of truth. *Narrative rationality* suggests ideas are truthful when they fit consistently into a culture's narrative history (supercontext). *Desire* is truthfully represented when the representational nature of meaning reveals itself.

The representative view invites questions about the ethics of speakers and audiences who are clearly implicated in the choices they make. The representative critic exposes the unexposed choices we make when we participate in meaning. Critical thinking gives us a moment to rethink our choices. It introduces possibilities into our own vision of meaning by identifying our ideas and the ideas of others, while reminding us that perhaps none of these ideas is absolutely true or essential.

Language is Identity, Knowing, and Acting

An equation between language, identity, knowing, and action assumes a much more fundamental role for language in the meaning of our lives. I will explain the equation by addressing the link between language and identity, knowledge, and then action. I could, however, start with any of these concepts and work my way to the others. Within this assumption, they are inextricable.

In order to grasp the significance of language to human identity, recall Jacques Lacan's position that language is necessary to human consciousness. Lacan argues that soon after babies become separate from their mothers, they use language to divide themselves into the self-conscious *I* that thinks and talks about *me*. In Lacanian terms, language is who we are. Lacan's profile of identity is a psychological profile that can be consistent with semiotic and metaphoric views of language as a mental process. The position that "we are" who "we speak" suggests critical thinkers can have a good deal more power over identity than those who assume identity is a given. Many critical concepts for studying meaning have been developed around this assumption and therefore work well together.

Style has been recovered from the representational assumption to support a vision that language defines people, their perceptions, and their actions. The functional view of style in particular asks how word choice constitutes reality.

Semiotics attempts to avoid a subject or object behind or in front of language, locating meaning in language. In the vocabulary of semiotics, identity and knowledge (knowing) are processes of using language to make distinctions. For instance, consider just one signifier that is often used to identify a professor, along with its first and second order signs. The person is carrying a "briefcase" which is an index that they are "carrying papers," and suggests an "air of importance." The identity of a professor is the act of distinguishing people who carry briefcases from people who carry paper bags, suitcases, or backpacks. Of course identity is more than a couple of signifiers. Critical thinkers use semiotics to explore the myths that attribute the briefcase with an air of importance, and combine it with other signifiers and myths used to characterize professors. Identity is an ongoing process of creating, maintaining, and changing sign systems.

Metaphors have also been equated with identity and knowing. Lakoff and Johnson's (1980) definition of metaphor calls attention to its cognitive dimension: "The essence of metaphor is **understanding** and **experiencing** one kind of thing in terms of another" (p. 6). They explain that language is metaphorical "precisely because there are metaphors in a person's conceptual system." (p. 5). The philosopher I. A. Richards (1965) argues that a metaphor is a process of borrowing and comparing thoughts, not shifting words (p. 94). For him, the metaphor is a cognitive/psychological process more than an expression of our psychology. The following quote from Richards (1965) addresses the way in which metaphor is a psychological, sometimes pathological, process:

> Metaphors can go deeper still into the control of the world that we make for ourselves to live in. The psycho-analysts have shown us with their discussions of 'transference'—another name for metaphor—how constantly modes of regarding, of loving, of acting, that have developed with one set

of things or people, are shifted to another. They have shown us chiefly the pathology of these transferences, cases in which . . . the borrowed attitude, the parental fixation, say—tyrannizes over the new situation . . . and behavior is inappropriate. . . . (p. 135)

The idea that metaphor is the center of thought and knowledge was a Renaissance Humanist idea that has been revived in the field of communication (Grassi, 1980). For example, Charles Darwin's "survival of the fittest" theory of evolution is believed to have come to him as a metaphorical transformation of the world of 19th century laissez-faire economics that he lived in. Johannes Kepler is said to have based his theory of planetary movements in musical movements.

Language that is who we are and what we know is an action. Language is an act because it brings people, cultures, and publics into being. Language is an action different from the motion of a physical reflex. As action, language involves choice, if even the choices are often subconscious (Burke, 1966, pp. 3-43). Language is also a social action, because even in the most innocuous forms, it works toward maintaining and/or challenging the order of our lives.

Equating language with identities, ideas, and action suggests an important role for critics of communication who can help us reconstruct who we are and what we know through language. Although this can be done with a variety of the concepts presented in this book, desire, identification, dramatic pentad, and narrative are concepts developed within this assumption. *Desire* most comfortably rests within the assumption, because it sends the critic to uncover the split identities established in, and then covered by, language. *Identification* takes place any time two or more ideas become consubstantial. The very act of using language identifies (is the same as) the substance of our experiences. Accordingly, metaphors and signs are processes of identification, as is all language. And recall, every act of identification is an act of division. Thus, similar to semiotics, the divisions or distinctions we make with language are necessary to meaning.

The terms of the *dramatic pentad* examine social realities—by considering the agents, acts, agency, scene, and purpose—that people enact in their communication. The pentad and the pentadic ratio direct the critic to consider the components in relationship to one another and in comparison to the possible dramas that were not enacted. Similarly, many critics claim human identities and knowledge only exist insofar as we have *narratives* that identify them. Remember that narratives are not just tales from storybooks but tales that structure most communication. History books tell stories. Talking science or religion is also narrative talk. The narrative form structures the meaning of our life-world (Fisher, 1984).

Critical Powers

The assumption that equates language, identity, knowing, and acting empowers the critic in most of the same ways as the representative assumption. There is one significant difference. In this view, language is fundamental to meaningful experiences. There is more room for the critical thinker to influence the meaning process. Critical thinking from within this perspective pays special attention to the distinctions, divisions, or "what is not" identified in language. This view is, therefore, well-suited to those interested in changing meanings or inventing new meanings. In the previous section, I stated that the representative view of language allows us to reconsider how our language represents ideas. We may or may not have the power to change what is being represented. When we equate language with reality, we can recreate ideas with a change in language. This view also asks the critic to suspend his or her own understanding of truth and to question truth from within and among language systems, which are ongoing and ever-changing.

In summary, centuries of philosophical thinking have not led to a unified or thorough explanation of how symbols relate to the world or our thoughts about ourselves and the world. There probably is not one true explanation, and if there were we might never know it, because philosophers, like all of us who use language, are limited by their own terministic screens. The communication critic evaluates how terministic screens might influence, express, represent, and/or constitute human identities, ideas, and actions. There are guidelines and concepts that oversee the process of thinking critically. This book has presented a vocabulary to help you analyze the context of communication and interpret the construction of meaning as you evaluate communication. But you do not really enter critical thinking until you reflect on your critical goals, your assumptions about communication, and how various critical tools fit with these assumptions and goals. Critical concepts are, after all, a critic's terministic screens.

Notes

1. The classical approach to educating the citizenry was organized into five canons: invention, memory, organization, style, and delivery. The canon of invention addresses the reasoning processes, emotions, and character of the communicators. The canon of memory, in classical times, concerned itself with how to remember ideas. Memory is now more broadly conceived as a collective history that shapes, and is shaped by, cultures. Organization, the third canon of study, is about how we structure ideas in thought and language. Style refers to language as it reflects the world, ideas about the world, and the "soul" of the speaker. Delivery, the final canon, describes how a speech is physically, vocally, and psychologically presented.

2. The difference is that cultural identities are by definition constructed in communication.

3. One can question the truth of language as expressive of identity but, in doing so, must assume that language also has other functions.

Reference List For Unit VII

Burke, K. (1966). *Language and symbolic action: Essays on life, literature, and method.* Berkeley: University of California Press.

Fisher, W. R. (1984). Narration as human communication paradigm: The case of public moral argument. *Communication Monographs, 51,* 1-22.

Grassi, E. (1980). *Rhetoric as philosophy: The humanist tradition.* University Park: Pennsylvania State University Press.

Hart, R.P. (1994). Wandering with rhetorical criticism. In W. L. Nothstine, C. Blair & G. A. Copeland (Eds.), *Critical questions: Invention, creativity, and the criticism of discourse and media* (pp. 71-81). New York: St. Martin's.

Hostettler, G. (1980). Speech as a liberal study II. *Communication Education, 29,* 332-347.

Isocrates (1956). *Antidosis.* (G. Norlin, Trans.). Cambridge, MA: Harvard University Press.

Lakoff, G., & Johnson, M. (1980). *Metaphors we live by.* Chicago, IL: University of Chicago Press.

Osborn, M. (1967). Archetypal metaphor in rhetoric: The light-dark family. *Quarterly Journal of Speech, 53,* 115-126.

Richards, I. A. (1965). *The philosophy of rhetoric.* New York: Galaxy.

GLOSSARY OF KEY CONCEPTS

Assumptions Ideas (beliefs, attitudes, values) that are not consciously supported with reasons. Assumptions may be explicitly stated or implied.

Camera Shot One, uninterrupted sequence of action recorded with one camera; also called a "cut." Cameras frame shots at varying distances and angles, with varying movements, and durations.

Character The person(s) or persona(s) shaped in and by communication. Ethos, second persona, and identification are three ways to think critically about character that are discussed in this book. See Narrative for a different sense of the concept, Character.

Conception/Conceptual Knowing The thought process through which people construct ideas. Conceptual knowing includes beliefs, attitudes, and values. See Perceptual Knowing.

Critical Thinking The process of systematically unraveling how people make meaning in communication. Thinking critically about communication involves an analysis of the communication context, an interpretation of how symbols come to have meaning in a given context, and an evaluation of the communication effectiveness, effects, truth, and/or ethics.

Culture   The symbolic processes through which people shape, share, reinforce, change, and pass on their ideas and ideologies. Overtime, we all participate in many cultures, including ethnicity, nationality, social class, and generation.

Cultural Power Struggles   Cultures compete for power over meaning in communication. A culture gains power when its ideas and means of making ideas dominate society.

Deduction   Formal, logical reasoning that moves from a statement called a major premise, through a statement called a minor premise, to a conclusion. See Syllogism and Validity.

Desire   A psychoanalytical concept that refers to a feeling of absence or lacking that turns to pleasure when fulfilled. See Form.

Discursive Formation   A social system that constrains the production of ideas with "governing rules" that determine who can communicate, what can be communicated, and how it must be communicated.

Dramatism or Dramatistic Perspective   A philosophical view of communication that claims people use symbolic behavior to enact the meaningful "realities" of our lives. See Pentad.

Editing   The ways images, sounds, and words are structured. This book only addresses the physical and technical process of visual editing.

Emotion   The feelings that are revealed, used, and/or created in communication. Pathos and desire are two ways to think critically about emotion that are discussed in this book.

Enthymeme   A form of rhetorical argument that reasons from popular and probable beliefs (not absolute truths) to probable claims. Because enthymemes are based on widely accepted beliefs, these beliefs are often implied rather than explicitly stated.

Ethos   The classical concept for the character of a speaker, as perceived by an audience. The concept can be used to think critically about the role of character in most communication.

Evidence Any idea that is used to support, prove, or justify another idea. Examples, statistics, factual data, testimony, and previously established or widely accepted beliefs are forms of evidence discussed in this book. Also called Data.

Example A rhetorical argument that reasons from one case to another case, through an inference that these cases are parallel. The term also refers to one type of evidence/data used in this form of argument; that is, a specific case or instance.

Field-Dependent Arguments Those arguments that must be evaluated within a particular field of expertise. The Toulmin model of argument (data, warrant, backing, qualifier, claim, rebuttal) is simply a way of diagramming the reasoning process so that it may be evaluated field dependently, according to the field that creates the backing for the warrant.

Form The psycho-symbolic process through which people use symbols to arouse and fulfill expectations.

Genre Any collection of communication texts which share symbolic strategies (in form and content) for responding to a recurring situation. Funeral orations, declarations of war, and torch songs are examples of communication genres.

Governing Rules Social rules that limit who can communicate, what they can communicate, and how they must communicate. Governing rules ultimately determine that which a society considers truthful and believable. See Discursive Formation.

Hailing A process of creating or imposing an identity in the ways we talk to others. For example, we hail children and adults differently; we are all hailed by friends, family, teachers, films, and books; we are often hailed according to/into cultural identities.

Ideas Perceptual and conceptual beliefs about ourselves, others, and the world.

Ideology A system of largely unquestioned ideas. Ideologies are unavoidable. Ideologies are oppressive to the extent they influence thought and action without any conscious reflection or choice.

Identification   The process of using language to become one with one's self, the universe, ideas, and/or other people. To identify is to overcome divisions and to unify with the substance of the other.

Identity (Identities)   Ideas we have about ourselves in relation to others and the world.

Induction   A form of logical reasoning that moves from evidence, through an inference, to a probable claim or conclusion.

Inference   The logical or rhetorical step in reasoning that connects one idea or statement (evidence or premise) to another idea or statement (conclusion). The study of logical reasoning distinguishes between inductive and deductive inferences.

Interpellated   The act of adopting or assuming the subject position necessary to make sense of a text. For instance, we are interpellated into the role of a consumer in television ads.

Language   All forms of expression, representation, or presentation (see chapter eighteen for philosophical distinctions) that come to have shared meanings for groups of people. Style, semiotics, and metaphors are three ways to look critically at language that are discussed in this book.

Logic   The formal and abstract process of deductive reasoning.

Metaphor   A figure of speech that states or implies that two distinct things are the same.

Motive   A concept used by dramatistic critics to describe a communicator's philosophical view of a situation. Critics uncover motives by first doing a pentadic analysis of communication and then determining which elements of the pentad control the drama. See Dramatism and Pentad.

Myth   The concept is used here as it is in semiotics; the pattern of beliefs, values, and/or attitudes that explain how a culture attaches a second order sign to a first order sign. For instance, a myth would explain how a culture attributes images of babies with purity.

Narrative   The structure of storytelling, typically ordered in time and may include a narrator, characters, setting, events, climax, and resolution. It is also a concept used by critics to interpret stories stated or implied in almost all communication. See Narrative Rationality.

Narrative Rationality   A term used to evaluate stories as reasoning, according to whether the stories are internally and externally consistent (narrative probability), and whether they are loyal to social values (narrative fidelity).

Organization   The classical concept for how people arrange ideas to effectively inform and persuade others through speech. The concept can be used to think critically about structure in most communication.

Pathos   The classical concept for the emotional dimensions of meaning. The concept can be used to think critically about emotion in most communication.

Pentad   A model used by dramatistic critics to interpret the ways people use language to construct a meaningful reality. The pentad, consisting of five parts (agent, act, scene, agency, purpose), is best used to examine the dramatic reality created by communication. See Dramatism.

Perception/Perceptual Knowing   The sensory processes through which people construct ideas. Perceptual knowing is seeing, hearing, touching, smelling, and tasting. Perceptual knowledge is commonly assumed to be factual knowledge. See Conceptual Knowing.

Point of View   The psychological perspective(s) through which the audience makes sense of a narrative. Often narrative structure invites the audience to identify with the point of view of a character in the drama. See Viewer Positioning.

Reasoning   The process of moving from one idea (evidence or data), to an unknown or unrecognized idea (claim or conclusion), through a third idea (inference or warrant). Rhetorical argument, field-dependent argument, and narrative rationality are three ways to think critically about reasoning that are discussed in this book.

Rhetoric   The formal and systematic study of persuasive, oral communication as it was developed in Classical Greek times (500 B.C.). Theories of rhetoric have been adapted to a variety of forms of communication since Classical times. The term *rhetoric* also refers to persuasive communication.

Rhetorical Argument   The classical concept for how people use reasoning to persuade others through speech. All rhetorical arguments are concluded with probability rather than certainty. The concept can be used to think critically about reasoning in most communication.

Rhetorical Situation   The context of purposeful communication. Rhetorical situations include exigencies that give rise to the communication, an audience that can potentially resolve the exigencies, and constraints that help or hinder the effectiveness of the communication in resolving the exigencies.

Scene   A shot or series of shots taken at the same location. See Pentad for a different sense of the concept, Scene.

Second Persona   The ideal audience (its attitudes, beliefs, and values) that is implied in communication.

Semiotics   The scientific study of language as systems of signs. See Sign.

Sequence   Two or more scenes that are linked by narrative theme, character, action, and/or time.

Sign   The concept is used here as it is in semiotics; A unit of meaning constructed of a signifier (image, color, sound, etc.) plus a first order (the symbolic, indexical, and/or iconic meaning attributed to the signifier) and second order (the valuative meaning attributed to the signifier) signified. Signs combine into systems of meaning, also called myths and ideologies.

Structure   The ways people put boundaries around ideas and/or things, and draw relationships between and among them. Organization, editing, narrative, and drama are four ways to look critically at structure that are discussed in this book.

Style   The classical concept for how people use words to effectively inform and persuade others through speech. The concept can be used to think critically about most communication.

Subject Position   A social and ideological identity that one must assume to participate in specific communication texts. Communication invites people to adopt a variety of subject positions. See Hailing, Interpellating, Viewer Positioning, and Point of View.

Supertext   The history of communication texts that become relevant to how people make sense of a text in a particular situation.

Syllogism   The formal structure of logical reasoning that moves from a statement about all cases, called a major premise; through a statement about all cases, called a minor premise; to a statement about a specific case or cases, called a conclusion. Syllogisms are concluded with certainty if the premises are true and the structure valid.

Terministic Screen   A filter that directs and deflects our perceptions and conceptions. All language is a terministic screen.

Valid/Validity   The formal consistency of syllogisms. Formal consistency or validity is determined by a set of universal logical rules.

Viewer Positioning   The way(s) in which camera shots, and editing, position the audience (in time and space) in relation to the images. Viewer positioning is a physical and technical process, but it often entails a social position.

Index

ABOUT THE AUTHOR

Jodi R. Cohen is an associate professor of speech communication at Ithaca College where she teaches courses in the practice, theory, and criticism of public communication. She received her B.A. and M.A. from Colorado State University in 1976 and 1979, respectively, and completed her Ph.D. at The Pennsylvania State University in 1984. Her research interests are communication and culture, communication and democracy, as well as critical studies of specific texts. Her works may be found in *Qualitative Inquiry, The Journal of Communication, Quarterly Journal of Speech, and Critical Studies in Mass Communication.*

2025